Deceptive Images

Deceptive Images

Toward a Redefinition of American Judaism

Charles S. Liebman

Transaction Books
New Brunswick (U.S.A.) and Oxford (U.K.)

Library of Congress Catalog Number: 88-1169
ISBN: 0-88738-218-5
Printed in the United States of America

Library of Congress Cataloging in Publication Data

Liebman, Charles S.
  Deceptive images.

  1. Judaism—United States—Historiography.
2. Jews—United States—Historiography.   3. Sociology,
Jewish—Historiography.   I. Title.
BM205.L539   1988   306′.6   88-1169
ISBN 0-88738-218-5

For Aunt Pearl,
Reut, and Elad

Contents

Contents

Preface

Readers may find that this volume falls short of being a book but I believe thay will agree that it is more than a collection of essays. It is based on some of my recently published articles which I chose because of their common themes. They all deal with my concern both as a social scientist and as a participant observer of American Jewish life with the manner in which American Jews and Judaism have been studied, and with my sensitivity to the policy implications of such studies. The first theme may find greater expression in one essay and the second theme in another although both themes are present in almost all of them. Nevertheless, I found it necessary to revise almost every essay as I turned each one into a chapter. I generally added new material in an effort to improve upon what I had written but I also tried to revise the material as best I could in order to produce an integrated book. I also sought to reduce overlap and repetition although I am aware of the fact that I have not been entirely successful in this effort

I do wish to acknowledge the publishers who have granted me permission to revise and reprint the original essays. Chapters one and seven were written expressly for this volume. Chapter two was originally published under the title "The Sociology of Religion and the Study of American Jews" in the May/June 1981 issue of *Conservative Judaism*. Chapter three was originally published under the title "Religious Extremism as a Religious Norm," in the March 1983 issue of the *Journal for the Scientific Study of Religion*. Chapter four appeared under the title "Orthodoxy Faces Modernity" in the Spring 1987 issue of *Orim*, a Jewish Journal at Yale. Chapter five first appeared as "The Debate on American Jewish Life: A Survivalist's Response to Some Recent 'Revisionist' Works," in volume four of *Studies in Contemporary Jewry* published by Oxford University Press (1987). Chapter six was published in monograph form by the American Jewish committee under the title *The Quality of Jewish Life*.

I suppose that anyone who writes about American Jews, however precise one may pretend to be and however careful in specifying which subgroup of American Jews one means, has someone specific in mind; someone who serves as a kind of implicit model. That is certainly true of myself. Whenever I generalize about American Jews—and I do so all too often, ignoring the obvious fact that there is no single type of American Jew—the implicit model against whom I judge the accuracy of what I say is my aunt, Mrs. Pearl Krieger. It is, therefore, appropriate that I dedicate this book to her. She shares the dedication with my two grandchildren, Reut and Elad. Both were born and are being raised in Israel. I hope that they will learn to share at least part of my passionate concern with American Jewry.

August, 1987 Petach Tikva

1

Introduction

Conflicting currents run through all the essays in this book. My deep concern for American Jewry is not entirely compatible with the detachment necessary for the social scientist seeking to describe American Jewish life. Nor, I confess am I an unreconstructed lover of all American Jews and of all things Jewish. I have a particular conception of what it means to be a Jew and although I would not attempt, even if I could succeed, to coerce all Jews into my Jewish mold, I do not view all manifestations of Jewishness with equanimity. It is very difficult to evaluate American Jewish life and various manifestations of Jewishness with objectivity when one passionately believes that some of these manifestations are harmful by one's personal criteria of Judaic propriety. It is all too easy to permit personal Judaic conceptions to overcome scientific responsibility. I would be foolish if I believed I had overcome this problem. But I have wrestled with it to the best of my ability. The opposite choice, studying that which one cares little about, raises problems of its own. It makes for dull research from the author's perspective and dull reading from the reader's perspective. More significantly, it makes for research that is often removed from reality, asks the wrong kinds of questions, and provides meaningless descriptions.

The second conflicting current reflects my own ambiguous feeling about social science, or at least my understanding of that professional discipline in which I have been trained. I am a social scientist. I think in social science categories, I describe events in terms of social science, I feel most comfortable in the company of other social scientists, and I identify with the profession of social science. On the other hand, I harbor a deep skepticism about the contributions of social science in the fields of sociology, political science and economics. They seem to me to have been rather meager. I have absolutely no faith in social science's predictive capacity and I have a measure of contempt for colleagues who take social science too seriously. "Too seriously," of course, means more seriously than I do. I do not pretend that my identity as a social scientist and my skepticism toward social science is compatible. If consistency is the hobgoblin of little minds my mind must be of gigantic capacity.

These conflicting currents pervade almost all the chapters. Nevertheless, the careful reader can discern the prevailing mood in which each was written: this despite my efforts at revision and integration. Chapters two and three are written from a social scientific perspective. In Chapter two I am concerned with describing what Jewish social scientists—by which I mean social scientists seeking to describe American Jewish life—can learn from concepts and theories drawn from the sociology of religion. This chapter is the most technical of all the chapters in the book and the general reader uninterested in sociology of religion might prefer to begin with chapter three. It is also the most dated. Since the core of the material was written in 1979 (though it was first published as an article in 1981) most of the literature cited in the chapter is from an earlier period. I only updated the endnotes where absolutely necessary. Those who do take the trouble to read the chapter, which does have much to say about how I think American Judaism ought to be studied, will be left with the feeling that my attitude toward the social sciences is unashamedly deferential. Chapter three dispels that impression. For in that chapter I suggest that social scientists might do well to rethink not only some of their assumptions but the very questions which they ask about religion. Extremism, I argue in that chapter, is misunderstood and misdiagnosed because it is not idiosyncratic but rather precisely what one should anticipate from a person who takes his religion seriously.

The remainder of the book reflects a more personal perspective. I rely heavily on concepts borrowed from the social sciences, but the topics also reflect my personal Jewish agenda. Chapter four begins with a critique of the social science literature as it applies to the study of Orthodox Judaism. Nevertheless, in my own effort to explain the survival of Orthodox Judaism I rely upon a key concept found in the work of Peter Berger. In addition, I also suggest that Conservative and Reform Jews and perhaps, by extension, religious liberals in general have something to learn from the way Orthodox Jews accommodate themselves to the modern environment.

Chapters five and six are efforts, sometimes polemical, to confront what I fear are dangerous tendencies in American Jewish life that find reinforcement among social scientists who study American Jewry. I refer to the current mood among American Jews to applaud the condition of American Jewish life. Along the way I also make clear some of my methodological biases in the study of American Jewry returning, in fact, to a theme first developed in the second chapter. Briefly, I believe that studies of American Jews have overemphasized the use of quantitative method and made far too little use of anthropological method. But my great concern in chapters five and six is that the policy implications implicit in the celebration of contemporary Jewish life in the United States are disastrous for its well being.

In chapter seven, the final chapter, I turn my attention specifically to the question of the policy implications in the contemporary study of American Jews. Chapter seven, in some respects, summarizes many of the points raised in prior chapters and it necessarily repeats some of the ideas presented there. That is virtually inevitable in a concluding chapter and deserves no apology.

2

The Sociology of Religion and the Study of American Jews

Jews in the United States are generally classified as a religious group. Paradoxically, they make use of concepts borrowed from a variety of social science disciplines to study themselves; but not concepts peculiar to the study of religious groups. They have relied on the fields of intergroup relations and minority group behavior or policy formation and interest group behavior. The key concepts have been: antisemitism, prejudice and discrimination or identity, acculturation and assimilation and more recently pressure group, lobbying and public opinion. Hardly any studies are informed by the sociology of religion. There are exceptions and Marshall Sklare's *Conservative Judaism*, which still remains the finest study of American Jewish life, is a notable one. But most studies of Jews make little explicit or even implicit use of the sociology of religion. Even those few studies which direct their attention to the internal aspects of Jewish life are more likely to rely on the literature of organizational behavior and/or decisionmaking than the sociology of religion.

One reason may be that there is no recognized field of study called American Jewish life. Students of contemporary American Judaism come from a variety of fields bringing with them the tools and theories of their particular disciplines. Hence, if students of American Jewish life haven't made use of the sociology of religion, perhaps the fault lies with that field. Why haven't its practitioners studied American Judaism? The question is a fair one but doesn't entirely account for the absence of religious sociology from American Jewish studies. Disciplines are not so hermetically sealed in the social sciences that a person in one field cannot inform himself about another. Secondly, increasing numbers of young people are entering the social sciences with a primary interest in learning more about Judaism. Hence, if they or older scholars choose to study Judaism from the perspective of interest group behavior or minority group relations it says some-

5

thing about the assumptions they make concerning what is or is not important in Jewish life. Sociology of religion plays such a small role in studies of American Jews, I believe, because students of American Jewish life don't consider the religious behavior of American Jews worthy of study. I also suspect that this bias has prevented their informing themselves about the concerns of the field.

I have two main points to make in this chapter. First, that the religious behavior of American Jews is critical to understanding American Jews. Secondly, that the sociology of religion has a great deal to say even to those who mistakenly believe that the religious behavior of American Jews is of trivial concern. I hope to accomplish my first objective by relying on some recent empirical studies of Jews. I hope to accomplish my second objective by surveying some of the recent, primarily theoretical literature in the sociology of religion.

Jewish Commitment and Religious Behavior

The American Jewish community is a voluntaristic one. The basic fact of American Jewish life is that the survival of American Judaism depends on the commitment and will of American Jews to survive. Consequently any understanding of American Jewish life must begin with questions of Jewish commitment, often mistakenly labeled as Jewish identity. Now, Jewish commitment is a mental construct. It is a label we attach to certain attitudes and behavior patterns. A moment's consideration suggests that there are many ways to measure Jewish commitment. One such measure is religious behavior; for example, belief in God, or the performance or the frequency of performance of such rituals as candle-lighting on Friday evening, celebration of a *seder*, synagogue attendance, observance of *kashrut*, and so on. Other measures of Jewish commitment might include: Jewish knowledge, continuing one's Jewish education, Jewish education of one's children, the proportion of one's friends or neighbors who are Jewish, Jewish philanthropic contributions, attitudes about Israel, concern for other Jews, attitudes toward intermarriage, and so on.[1]

The most striking finding in research on Jewish commitment is that the various measures are related, and the most powerful of these is religious behavior. This is found in studies of attachment to and identity with Israel[2] (which, by the way, is no less true for Jews outside the United States[3]), in studies of Jewish philanthropy,[4] of Jewish apostasy, that is, accounting for those people born Jewish who no longer identify themselves as Jews,[5] and for studies measuring Jewish commitment according to a variety of indices with a variety of consequences.[6] Furthermore, there is a correlation between religious commitment and denominational identification. Orthodox

Jews score higher on indices of religious behavior and belief than do Conservative Jews, Conservative Jews higher than Reform Jews, and Reform Jews higher than Jews who don't identify themselves by denomination or who choose to call themselves "just-a-Jew."[7] Of course there are individual exceptions. But among groups of American Jews the evidence is clear. Socio-demographic factors such as age, income, education, how many generations have been in the United States, geographic location, and so on are related to the various measures of Jewish commitment. But the best single measure of Jewish commitment, however one chooses to define it, is religious commitment. In addition, the synagogue is the Jewish institution with which the greatest number of American Jews are affiliated and the unaffiliated are unlikely to belong to other organizations with the possible exception of Jewish community centers.[8]

All this suggests that the religious behavior of American Jews is absolutely critical in understanding other aspects of their behavior. Even if one proceeds from the perspective of a complete secularist, even if one believes that religion is doomed, that Jews are really a nation or an ethnic group or a culture and therefore, Judaism can survive without religion, that synagogue affiliation and even attendance or other ritual behavior is trivial because it engages so few Jews and is of little obvious consequence—the study of the religious behavior of American Jews remains central to a study of American Judaism. It doesn't really matter what the researcher thinks about religion or even what respondents report about the implications of religion in their lives. One cannot overlook the religious factor because, as the previous discussion suggests, it is so critical in defining the essence of being Jewish. By overlooking the religious factor one doesn't know if one is studying Jewish behavior or behavior that happens to characterize American Jews and which can be accounted for by any number of other variables such as class, education, occupation or income. But if it is conceded that religion, defined in the narrowest categories of religious belief and behavior or synagogue affiliation, is critical in understanding Jewish behavior and therefore merits study, it follows that one will look to the field of sociology of religion for insights, for methodological tools and for evidence about the correlates and consequences of religious commitment and developments in the world of religion. I will also argue that some formulations in the theoretical area of the sociology of religion can be helpful beyond that which I have suggested.

The Theoretical Tradition[9]

One strain in the sociology of religion traces its origins to concerns of specific religious institutions with their "market research" orientation. Religious groups want to know the number of their adherents, the locations of their churches and members, and the social characteristics and/or the nature of their adherents' beliefs. Market research type studies have expanded beyond the needs of client organizations. A host of studies have tested the relationship between socio-economic status and religious affiliation or socio-economic status and sectarian or fundamentalist beliefs and behavior.[10] Most studies find that the higher one's socio-economic status the more likely one is to be religiously affiliated, but among the affiliated, the lower the socio-economic status the more likely one is to be a fundamentalist in belief and behavior. Some of these studies proceeded, implicitly or explicitly, from hypotheses generated from the work of Max Weber, although the researchers' assumptions were sometimes simplistic, their understanding of religion rather shallow, and their techniques identical to those in the narrower "market research" field. Other studies sought to trace the consequences of religious belief and behavior.[11] Finally, a most popular type of study has been the description of contemporary cults, third world religions and the growth of charismatic, pentecostal and fundamentalist tendencies within established religions.[12]

My interest here is not with these studies. Instead, I want to discuss a second strain in the sociology of religion which stems from central concerns in the study of society. Indeed, the classical sociologists of religion began with an interest in man and society, not religion. The concerns of the classicists with social organization and the human condition led them to consider religion as a crucial, if not *the* crucial, dimension of human culture.[13] Those concerned with theory have, by and large, continued to argue for the important place of religion in society even when they believed it was in decline in industrial societies.[14] How could they do so?

One method is to argue with the interpretation of the data, to select aspects which support a contrary opinion, or to dispute the validity and reliability of the data. Andrew Greeley is a most skillful exemplar of this method.[15] Greeley argues that modern man is no less religious today, that religion is not in decline, that secularism is not the wave of the future. It is important to remind ourselves that just as not everybody was religiously committed in the past so not everyone is religiously indifferent today. Roughly one-third of the population in Great Britain and the United States report religious experiences and not all of this group are church attenders.[16]

The second method is to redefine religion.[17] If church attendance, religious faith and the perceived consequences of religion in the adherents' life are declining, perhaps this only indicates a decline of institutional religion, not religion itself.[18]

There are two distinguishable, though related, lines to this argument. One line is the functionalist approach. Functionalists argue that religion cannot be defined by the substance of religious beliefs and practices since there is no belief or practice that all groups commonly thought of as religions share, including a belief in God. They would substitute a functionalist definition. That is, they would define religion by the function which it performs in society. Once a functional definition is adopted one can argue that even if institutional religion, i.e., the Church or the Synagogue ceases to perform its function, other agencies within society may replace them. A functionalist definition of religion permits one to argue for the centrality of religion despite the evidence for its institutional decline. Thomas Luckmann, for example, argues that religion is so basic that one can no more conceive of a society or man without religion than a society without politics or economics.[19]

Luckmann's particular understanding of religion is also associated with a second group of thinkers who assert the continued importance of religion for society. They share the conception of religion as a set of symbols which relate man to the ultimate conditions of existence. I don't think that either the functional or the substantive label is quite appropriate to such a definition, although at least one member, Peter Berger, classifies himself as a substantivist. Implicit in this definition is the possibility that religious symbol systems need not necessarily be embedded in such institutional frameworks as the Church or Synagogue. But the fact that these "religious" institutions are so closely associated with core religious symbols means that people are more likely to renew their institutions or to add new symbols within traditional institutional frameworks than to abandon these institutions. Some define religion in explicitly substantive terms (e.g., symbol systems pertaining to beliefs in mystical or supernatural powers), but then go on to distinguish sacred symbols. Sacred is not only that which is special and set apart, but also that which is unquestioned. Hence, whereas all religious symbols are sacred, not all sacred symbols (for example a flag) are religious. In this case, even if religious symbols are no longer important to society, sacred symbols are.

This second group of thinkers to whom I have referred doesn't represent a school of thought, though all its members draw upon the work of Alfred Schutz who was concerned with the nature of social reality.[20] There are certainly differences between the members. The presentation that follows is a distillation of their thought and does not reflect the thinking of any one member.

The key concepts in this group's understanding of religion are: meaning, culture and symbol. I shall try to explain what they mean by each concept.

Man seeks meaning. That is, he seeks a sense of purpose, an understanding of who he is, of his role in life, of assurance that what he does and what he experiences transcends the immediate and the sensory. Otherwise, for example, the suffering man undergoes, or the knowledge of his own mortality would plunge him into despair. Human relationships, for example, would sour because they would be perceived as governed only by immediate needs. Neither friendship nor family have a place in a world where life or activity or experience do not interrelate in any meaningful pattern, where the relationship itself is not grounded in some ultimate sense of rightness.

Family relations provide both example and paradigm for the preceeding concept. The traditional concept of family encompasses a variety of types of obligatory relationships between, for example, husband and wife or parent and child. These are based on the assurance that family is rooted in the very nature of life, complying in some way with the order of the universe. The family crisis which we are experiencing results, in part, from the breakdown of the *meaning* of family and its transformation into a set of contractual relationships based on the expectation of advantages to be gained from entering into and perpetuating the relationship. Once the balance of advantages and disadvantages shifts to one's disfavor, commitments to family cease being obligatory and for example, one side or the other will decide it wants a divorce or will feel entitled to desert the family.

Religion serves to strengthen family life by legitimating its ultimate meaning, rooting it in ultimate reality. It does this by embedding familistic behavior in law whose source is a transcendent authority, by binding family members together through ritual which is celebrated together and by conveying the image of the family and its importance in myth.

Meaning is not the same as cognitive understanding. Cognitive understanding is only necessary for those who question the meaning of life. Few of us do because we are raised from early childhood with implicit assurances that life does have meaning. Indeed, in all likelihood no rational explanation of the meaning of life (assuming such an explanation could be given) would satisfy someone who ceased to believe in that meaning, whose own perceptions of reality no longer reinforced the assumptions that life had meaning.

Culture is the system of inherited conceptions of meaning expressed in symbols through which men communicate, and perpetuate and develop their knowledge about, and attitudes toward, life. Symbols are the vehicles of cultural expression. They stand for patterns because they are perceived as being part of the reality which they signify. In Geertz's terms, they are models *of* as well as models *for*.[21]

Let me illustrate the meaning of the concept *symbol* with an example of an important American Jewish symbol; really a subset of symbols—New York's Lower East Side. If American Jews have any sacred history it is surely the history of the Lower East Side of New York at the beginning of this century and to a lesser extent its counterparts in other urban areas. If it is not a religious symbol it comes very close to being one. Like all symbols it can mean different things to different people. It can even contain contradictory meanings and it remains open to new meanings. Surely, among its most important meanings are: hard work yields success, education is a basic Jewish value, Jews have suffered in the United States, the United States is the land of opportunity for those willing to work, Jews will succeed regardless of how tough conditions are. But the Lower East Side is more than any one or all of these meanings. It evokes a sense of awe and triggers a sense of Jewish belongingness and community as well as a sense of family because it points to genesis, to origins.

Religion is that set of symbols which roots cultural conceptions into the general order of the universe. This is what makes the symbols sacred. But precisely because religion is expressed symbolically, it shapes our conceptions of meaning as it legitimates them. To return to the example of family, religion legitimates family relations by assuring us that family is part of the general order of the universe. Thus, for example, the biblical story of Adam and Eve as a mythic symbol or the *seder* as a ritual symbol serves these roles, among others. Each not only legitimates the family but conveys models for particular types of family relationships. A good example of a specifically religious Jewish symbol is *kashrut*. Among its other meanings *kashrut* points to Jewish distinctiveness and separation. As Mary Douglas points out, our body and the ritualized uses we make of our body are symbols of our relationship to society. Emphasis on what we ingest, what we take into our body, symbolizes the emphasis on distinctions between ourselves and the outer society. It suggests separation from others. *Kashrut* is a statement about relations between Jew and non-Jew and participation in the ritual of *kashrut* enforces this separation, both socially and perceptually.

I am most partial to the conception of religion as a system of meaning. Nevertheless, I believe that the works of the thinkers whom I have described have two serious shortcomings. First, I don't think their work clarifies the boundaries between religious and non-religious symbols. In practice, they are often indistinguishable but analytically the boundaries ought to be clearer. Second, there is an anthropological and/or Protestant bias in the conception of religion which places so little emphasis on what any devout Jew or Muslim and perhaps even Catholic experiences as being of central importance in religion; the fact is that religion provides normative prescriptions of behavior. It tells one what to do. It is a system of law. Now this conception of religion can be incorporated into the formulation of religion as a meaning system but it seems to me that if a Jew or Muslim were undertaking a definition of religion the normative realm would receive more explicit formulation. Furthermore, if religion is a system of law, it is not mediated entirely through symbol.[22]

Beyond Institutions

Religion need not necessarily be institutionalized. That is, we can conceive of religion as a set of symbols diffused within a culture which conveys meaning or legitimates systems of belief without a distinctive hierarchical organization, an elite or an explicit structure. Religion was diffused rather than institutionalized in ancient Chinese culture. Those who talk of civil religion or political religion imply that a similar phenomenon may also be present in contemporary society. In fact, it can be argued that only diffuse religion is pure religion. Institutionalized religion means something more and something less than religion as a system of meaning. It means something more because an institution generates its own needs, its own self interests, its own elaboration which may exist quite independently of its function. Hence, we cannot understand institutional religion without knowing a great deal about its recruitment procedures, personnel, finances, authority system, adherents, allies, relationships to other social institutions, and so on. All of this will be more or less related to its role in provision of meaning but is clearly not the heart of the religious phenomenon. Obviously one task for the sociologist of religion is to relate these aspects of the religious institution to religion. Unfortunately, some empirical studies of religion concern themselves with the institutional or organizational aspects without noting in what ways, if any, they interrelate with "religion," i.e., in what ways aspects such as "power" or "hierarchy" which characterize all institutions relate to beliefs or symbols which are distinctive to a particular religious group.[23]

On the other hand, institutional religion may be something less than religion because other institutions may also provide and legitimate systems of meaning for an individual. One thinks, in particular, of professions, business corporations, some political groups, leisure time associations and, in a less institutionalized form, of age groups—particularly the young and the elderly.

But there is yet another way in which we may say that religion shares in the provision and legitimation of meaning with other facets of culture. Religion, whether it is diffuse or institutionalized, is a perspective, a way of viewing reality. We conduct our lives, for the most part, through reliance on common sense. This common sense, the taken-for-granted aspect of behavior and experience, may be informed by, rooted in, or derived from some ultimate religious belief, but most of us are certainly not conscious of this in our daily activity. Rather, we are most conscious of transcendence and turn to religion at those moments when common sense no longer provides adequate meaning, when routinized responses no longer suffice to provide understanding and events seem to challenge the very assumptions on which our lives are built. This may occur as a result of our own particular experiences—birth, death, other rites of passage—or by social crises, or it may be generated by the religious institution itself through special days or ceremonies which remind us of the contingency and precariousness of our every day common-sensical world and world views.

Another related way of viewing religion as sharing in the provision of meaning is suggested by Victor Turner's analysis.[24] He emphasizes religion as a liminoid or threshold type experience which stands in opposition to everyday experience. His studies suggest that the relation of religion to common sense may parallel the relationship of what he calls *communitas* to social structure. Society is comprised of structured roles which provide the organization, hierarchy, division of labor, and authority system necessary to survive. But this social structure, characterized by heterogeneity, inequality, status and partiality may distort a sense of the basic wholeness of society, the sense of kinship and mutuality. Borrowing "I-thou" conceptions from Buber, Turner suggests the need for liminoid experiences, which affirm the homogeneity, equality, absence of status and wholeness of a community. As the participant undergoes the liminoid experience, as he feels himself totally integrated into a community, he senses that the norms which govern structural relationships are dissolved. This, in turn, is accompanied by the feeling of power and the liberation of new energy. The liminoid experience, by breaking down social distances and structures temporarily, is "a transformative experience that goes to the root of each person's being and finds in that root something profoundly communal and shared."[25] Turner's discussion of contemporary religion points to the possibility that the major role of religion today is in the provision of this liminoid experience. Hippie communes popularized in the seventies and other utopian experiments represent efforts to establish and extend the liminoid experience into permanent forms of living. They also evoke, at least in part, associations with the increasingly popular Jewish *havurot*.

Religion viewed as a meaning system raises a number of questions about American Judaism. What is the Jewish meaning system as it is projected in ceremonial observances, the American synagogues (which differ among themselves), Jewish schools, rabbinic sermons, prayerbooks, the Jewish press, statements by Jewish leaders, Jewish fiction, and so on? Is it only symbols themselves or what the symbols refer to which distinguishes American Judaism from American Protestantism or Catholicism? Clearly, there is no simple answer to this question. But if we know little about the answer it indicates to me that we know very little about American Jews.

Marshall Sklare has been among the few who have posed the question. But Sklare's achievement is flawed by the fact that he does not pose it explicitly or theoretically and does not, therefore, explore the problem in all its ramifications or specify those aspects of the problem which he does explore. For example, we want to know whether, where and how American Judaism is speaking to the universal condition of man who happens to be Jewish or the specific condition of Jewishness. The two are not the same today though they may once have been. The sociology of religion alerts us to seek the answer initially in those Jewish symbols which evoke the greatest resonance. Israel and the Holocaust are the regnant Jewish symbols. This not only suggests that American Jewish meaning systems are rather particularistic but how difficult it is to distinguish Jewish religion from Jewish ethnicity when one necessarily evokes the other in symbolic terms. The power of symbols is in their openness, their capacity to absorb new meanings and to express various levels of meaning drawn from various domains of social experience and normative evaluations. Neither Israel nor the Holocaust need necessarily point to exclusively ethnic or parochial concerns though I suspect they do for most Jews.

Religious Ritual

We have observed that religion is composed of beliefs and practices which are conveyed and expressed primarily through symbols. The major symbols through which religion is conveyed are rituals and myths.

Rituals serve a variety of functions as students of the subject have indicated.[26] First of all, they are intrinsically proper. In other words, by performing a ritual the adherent does what he is supposed to do. By not performing a ritual one is behaving improperly. But the source which makes behavior proper or improper is the source of all power and authority. Hence, even when the adherent is unaware of this, the ritual performance itself assures him that there is an order and that he is part of that order.

This is closely connected to a second function of ritual. It is a way of relating the performer to the ultimate source of meaning—to God. In one sense, as we just noted, all ritual does this. But some rituals are especially geared to reinforcing this relationship. One thinks of prayer, or of those rituals which reenact historically rooted religious experiences thereby recalling a sense of the immediacy of God.

Thirdly, ritual is efficacious. The proper performance of ritual is necessary or at least helpful in bringing about certain outcomes whether they be of a private or public nature. Fourth, rituals serve as evocative devices. They arouse and channel but also sublimate and control such strong emotions as anger, grief, love, hate, and so on.

Fifth, ritual is a way of organizing perceptions of reality of the physical and social world. This may be the world as experienced or the world as it ought to be and, therefore, as it exists in some prefiguration or in God's mind or as it will be.

Finally, ritual serves a communal function. An increasingly self-conscious religious laity seems to be quite self-conscious about this. Ritual, especially when celebrated with others, evokes the sense of ties to community, the community of the present and the past, and strengthens one's sense of dependence on and obligation to that community. Analysis of ritual is not confined to the explication of the cognitive referents of its symbols. It includes the analysis of bodily motion, of space and distance, of timing.[27] It is hardly an exact science but applications of its method to contemporary settings are, at the very least, highly suggestive of what the participants are trying to do and feel and say even if they are unaware of it.

Individuals and societies differ in the importance they ascribe to religious ritual. Explaining what relationship if any exists between ritual and social structure is certainly a major task for the sociology of religion. The most important work on this topic is Mary Douglas' *Natural Symbols.*[28] Douglas proceeds from the insight of Durkheim that the idea of God is constituted from the idea of society. Society is something that we apprehend though we do not experience it with our senses. We nevertheless "know" that it encompasses us, shapes our lives, determines that which is right and wrong. According to Durkheim, our conception of God emerges from our experience of society. Religion enables us to reify society so that we can relate to it meaningfully. Douglas is concerned with the ritual expressions of the relationships between man and society, and particularly man's use of his own body as a symbolic representation of his perception of society. Ritual expresses our sense of order. In those cultures where man perceives himself as intimately related to society, lacking autonomy and individual freedom, where the social group grips its members in tight communal bonds, ritual is most highly developed, and symbolic action is perceived as efficacious. Individual autonomy, the breakdown of the individual's sense of group dependence, means a movement away from ritual and toward greater ethical concern.

Relying on the work of Basil Bernstein, Douglas describes two types of family systems in our culture which produce different orientations to ritual in the child. One family is called "positional." In this family the child is controlled by a sense of social pattern. He is told he must do things or cannot do things because of a given structure—his age, his sex, his place in the family hierarchy. A child who rebels against such a system is made to feel he is challenging his very culture.

The contrast to the positional family is the "personal" family. Here stress is laid on the unique value of every individual. Questions are answered by reference to the consequences of actions. Behavior is controlled by sensitizing the child to the feelings of others through an analogy with his own feelings. ("You can't do something because .... 'it would worry your Mother' or 'because I've got a headache' or 'how would you feel if you were a cat?'") In other words, control is exercised through person-oriented appeals. The child of the personal family is not a prisoner of cultural position but of feelings and abstract principles:

> The child is being educated for a changing social environment. As his parents move from one town or country to another in response to the need for professional mobility, the child grows in a family system which is relatively unstructured, a collection of unique feelings and needs. Right and wrong are learnt in terms of his response to those feelings. Instead of internalizing any particular social structure his inside is continually stirred into a ferment of ethical sensibilities. We can immediately and from our own experience recognize this as the basis for the move from ritual to ethics.[29]

Douglas argues that pressures of home and school which result in child-rearing practices of this type predispose one to ethical concerns, open up a vocabulary of feelings, but deny the child a sense of pattern to his social life. The child must now look for justification of his existence outside the performance of set rules. He finds this justification in good works on behalf of humanity, or in personal success, or both.

The personal family emphasizes verbal elaboration and an impersonal language, the use of words whose meanings are objective, universal, unburdened by emotional or personal or group overtones. Success in the modern world depends on the individual's ability to utilize these modes of unambiguous communication rather than symbols which are always rooted in a particular culture. The paradox, however, is that:

> ... social responsibility is no substitute for symbolic forms and indeed depends upon them. When ritualization is openly despised the philanthropic impulse is in danger of defeating itself. For it is an illusion to suppose that there can be organization without symbolic expression . . . Those who despise ritual, even at its most magical, are cherishing in the name of reason a very irrational concept of communication.[30]

Let me cite one instance where I find Douglas' study most helpful in understanding contemporary American Judaism. I have often wondered about the relative success of the Orthodox in transmitting certain behavior patterns towards which some Conservative Jews have no less a commitment. Let us take the example of *kashrut*. Granted, a much smaller percentage of Jews who identify themselves as Conservative observe laws of *kashrut* however they define them, than do Orthodox Jews. But my personal observations suggest that even in those Conservative homes where *kashrut* is extremely important, grown children are less likely to observe *kashrut* than those raised in Orthodox homes. A reading of Douglas suggests that this may be related to a sense of community. A crucial difference between the Conservative home and Orthodox home is the Jewish community into which each is related. The Orthodox home is related to a *kashrut*-observing community of time and place. The Orthodox Jew lives with the sense of an omnipresent community which mediates relationships to other Jews, to Jewish history, and to major Jewish symbols. At the simplest level this means that relationships to the local Jewish community, the national Jewish community and even to Israel takes place through a network of institutions (the synagogue, the day school, American counterparts of Israeli political parties, hospitals and other philanthropic societies, and so on) which share an Orthodox orientation. On the other hand, relationships at the most intimate level, family and peers, are, at least to some extent, governed by a sense of obligation toward the rules and customs of that community. The same sense of community governs relationships to the Jewish past. Now this has a double reinforcing effect. Precisely because of the omnipresent sense of community, the notion of ritual and the efficacy of ritual, as Douglas suggests, is natural rather than artificial. Gripped in the web of community bonds, both in a metaphysical as well as a material sense, the Orthodox Jew *believes* because he *experiences*. Moreover, the specific injunctions of the community such as *kashrut* observance are backed by sanctions of community favor or disfavor, approval or disapproval.

Even the best Conservative homes often lack this type of linkage to a Jewish community. Their Jewish community is, on the one hand, far more ephemeral and permeable, less omnipresent than that of the Orthodox Jew. Hence, not only are its rules less compelling but rules are not natural. Secondly, the Jewish community to which the Conservative home is linked is not a *kashrut*-observing community. This is not only true in the specific sense that these extended family and peer groups are less likely to be *kashrut*-observing than those among the Orthodox, but in the broader sense that the Conservative home is linked to the broader Jewish community through non-Conservative institutions, institutions to whom *kashrut* is irrelevant. Israel, for example, is the preeminent symbol of Jewish life. The Conservative home relates to Israel without the mediation of *kashrut*-observing institutions. *Kashrut*, in other words, is irrelevant in the most Jewishly significant activity which the Conservative home undertakes. One wonders whether this may not even be true of the relationship of that home to the Jewish tradition. Is the relationship mediated by the symbols of Torah and Sinai with their overtly religious connotation or is it mediated through conceptions of Jewish history and shared destiny with their more secular and ethnic overtones?

Douglas' study suggests the importance of institutions such as the Conservative movement's Camp Ramah or United Synagogue Youth which provide broader linkages for young people and thereby combat the sense that traditional Jewish orientations are exclusively familistic or private.

Religious Myth

Perhaps because the term myth has such strong associations with ancient cosmological stories, sociologists of religion have not explored its function and meaning for contemporary man. An unintended consequence of the work of such important contemporary scholars as Claude Levi-Strauss or Mircea Eliade has been to reinforce the association of myth with primitive stories.[31] Nor has there been much help from other disciplines.[32]

Myth has been defined as "the expression of unobservable realities in terms of observable phenomena."[33] In another study I try to indicate the central role of myth in the construction of Israeli society by analyzing the stories of Tel-Ḥai, Massada and the Holocaust and indicating how they are experienced through as well as reinforced by older myths.[34] Exploring the myths of contemporary American Jewry should be most instructive. Myth, like ritual, can be explored exegetically with emphasis on what the story relates and the different meanings contained in the story, or it can be analyzed structurally. The latter type of analysis which owes so much to the work of Levi-Strauss is most difficult to undertake in the case of contemporary myth. Nevertheless, one can study the types of protagonists, the levels of relationships that exist between them, the use of names, and so on. At the exegetical level the analysis is more obvious and is likely to yield more demonstrable conclusions. For example, let us take the myth of New York's Lower East Side. What is it that Jews choose to tell one another and non-Jews about Jewish life there? Clearly, American Jews are projecting images of themselves as they tell the story of their origins. What do they emphasize and what do they omit in their Hebrew school texts, organizational literature, and fiction? Alternatively, how do American Jews recount the stories of the Jewish holidays and in what ways, if any, does their recounting differ from other Jewish versions? Unfortunately, we have no such studies.

Religious and Secular

The analysis of myth and ritual, as we have seen, may be extended to activity that is not generally defined within the sphere of religion. In fact, sociologists of religion have turned their attention in recent years to the importance of religious or quasi-religious symbols in secular contexts. If influence is measured by attentiveness, response, and inspiration for further research then the most influential article in the sociology of religion in the last two decades is Robert N. Bellah's "Civil Religion in America."[35] Bellah's argument is that "there is a collection of beliefs, symbols and rituals with respect to sacred things and institutionalized in a collectivity"[36] whose concern is the American experience and which exists independently of the institutionalized religions of America. We have already noted that religion provides its adherents with meaning. It serves man's need to order his environment and his experiences and to support his "efforts to survive in a world of scarce resources, abundant perils and endless suffering."[37] But it may also reflect, sustain and legitimize the social order. Beginning with Bellah's essay, increasing attention has been devoted to symbol systems which provide sacred legitimation of the social order under the label of civil or civic religion.

It seems superfluous to suggest the utility of the civil religion concept in analyzing the activity of Jewish secular organizations, in particular, Jewish Federations. A fine example is the work of Jonathan Woocher whose study is discussed again in the final chapter of this book.[38] Woocher argues that Federation activities reflect a system of beliefs and rituals which form a civil religion by structuring the relationship of the Jewish political system in the United States to the realm of the sacred. While this civil religion overlaps with the Judaism of the synagogue, it is civil Judaism that serves as a common faith of American Jews. Civil Judaism, Woocher maintains, not only functions like a religion but is substantively religious because its characteristic beliefs, values and symbols point to a transcendent (suprarational) source of meaning for the activity of the Jewish polity. Woocher then documents his assertion with citations from statements by Federation leaders. He summarizes the faith of civil Judaism in a number of tenets whose ethos and world view is activist, communal and this worldly, affirming the reality and the saliency of the distinction between Jews and non-Jews while continuing to hold universalistic ideals. He notes the important role of such terms as "messianic" and "destiny" in civil Judaism, terms which point to its transcendent dimension. But major elements of traditional Judaism are absent and/or transformed. Thus, for example, Torah and halakha become the "tradition" or the "cultural heritage" and *mitzvot* become "Jewish ethics," and I would add, "giving." The quest for holiness becomes the quest for "quality" and "excellence" in Jewish life and the active choosing God becomes the activist and responsible Jewish community.

Conclusions

The role of the religious elite, of religious leaders, has always been to convey the particular meaning of religion, to impose religious experiences by participation in religious acts, to teach the adherent to manipulate the religious symbols. But contemporary religious leaders must also explicate the points of contact between the religious and the common sense meanings of life. The role of the sociologist of religion is to relate religious meaning and religious expression to social, structural and psychological processes. This kind of information, at least for some, legitimates movement from the common sense realm to the religious realm by making it comprehensible. In other words, I am suggesting that the language and perspectives of social science may offer a bridge to move from the everyday to the sacred. In a "religious" age, or among some type of people—the very young, the very deviant, the very skeptical, the very alienated, the very romantic and mystical—the common sense world may be so devoid of meaning, or the religious world so pregnant with meaning that the latter need not be legitimated in terms of the former. But, for most of us, if the religious world is to serve as more than a temporary refuge from the really real and really relevant, connections have to be made in terms that are comprehensible in the language of the everyday world.

The fact that religion requires legitimation in language drawn from the non-religious realm suggests its difficulty with contemporary culture. It is in this sense that religion is in decline. It is not religion itself that must be made intelligible in the everyday sense of that term. That is impossible. It is a contradiction in terms. Rather, the religious impulse, the religious activity, the act of doing religion requires explication. And it is at this point that the sociologist of religion can be of assistance.

The best of the sociology of religion literature provides theory and insight which helps us understand behavior as it is embedded in social and psychological structures of society. It also permits us to borrow its findings in the analysis of quasi-religious manifestations in non-religious realms. It makes no claim to reduce religious symbols to social or psychological categories. Rather, it makes explicable in one language and one realm, activity which is only experienced in another language and another realm. To this extent, it not only provides the major theoretical schema for understanding American Judaism but it may become an instrument helpful in shaping programs conducive to Jewish survival.

Notes

1. Bernard Lazerwitz has done the most extensive work in developing indices of Jewish commitment. See, for example, "Religious Identification and Its Ethnic

Correlates," *Social Forces* 52 (December 1973):204–222. Sociologists of religion have devoted a great deal of attention in recent years to measures of religious commitment. The most widely accepted measures are: ideology or belief, private religious experience and devotion, knowledge, and ritual behavior. A summary of the literature is found in Ronald C. Wimberley, "Dimensions of Commitment: Generalizing from Religion to Politics," *Journal for the Scientific Study of Religion* 17 (September 1978):225–240.

2. Marshal Sklare and Joseph Greenblum, *Jewish Identity on the Suburban Frontier* (New York: Basic Books, 1967), pp. 231–234; Bernard Lazerwitz, "Some Jewish Reactions to the Six Day War," *Reconstructionist* 34 (November 8, 1967):23.

3. Doris Bensimon-Donat, "North African Jews in France," *Dispersion and Unity* 10 (Winter 1970):124–126. The correlation between religious commitment and attachment to Israel is even found among Israeli youth. Simon Herman, *Jewish Identity: A Social Psychological Perspective* (Beverly Hills: Sage, 1977), pp. 187–191, 197–201.

4. Steven M. Cohen, "Will Jews Keep Giving? Prospects for the Jewish Charitable Community," *Journal of Jewish Communal Service* 55 (Autumn 1978):59–71. The paper is based on a secondary analysis of the 1975 survey of Jews in metropolitan Boston.

5. David Caplovitz and Fred Sherrow, *The Religious Drop-Outs: Apostasy Among College Graduates* (Beverly Hills: Sage, 1977), pp. 97–105.

6. Harold S. Himmelfarb, "Patterns of Assimilation-Identification Among American Jews," paper presented to the Seventh World Congress of Jewish Studies, Jerusalem, Israel, 1977; Bernard Lazerwitz "An Approach to the Components and Consequences of Jewish Identification," *Contemporary Jewry* 4 (Spring/Summer 1978):3–8.

7. Bernard Lazerwitz and Michael Harrison, "American Jewish Denominations: A Social and Religious Profile," *American Sociological Review* 44 (August 1979): 656–666. See also, Charles S. Liebman, *The Ambivalent American Jew* (Philadelphia: Jewish Publication Society, 1973), pp. 142–143 and the literature cited therein. Less clear is whether denominational affiliation operates independently of religious behavior. That is, are Orthodox Jews more likely to be Jewishly committed than Conservative Jews, or Conservative Jews more than Reform Jews even if their level of ritual observances is identical? I suspect the answer is yes if for no other reason than peer group and reference group expectations and pressures.

8. Charles S. Liebman, "American Jewry: Identity and Affiliation," in *The Future of the Jewish Community in America* ed. David Sidorsky (New York: Basic Books, 1973), pp. 142–144.

9. I intend to discuss the contributions of a number of anthropologists of religion without distinguishing them from sociologists. In fact, those aspects which I will emphasize are points of convergence between the two disciplines. Durkheim, Weber, Freud and Malinowski are the intellectual progenitors for theoreticians in both fields. By and large, it seems to me that those trained in sociology are concerned with the role of religion in society and hence with the boundaries of religion whereas the anthropologists take this role for granted and exhibit greater concern with an analysis of the structure of the religious symbol or the religious act. There are, of course, exceptions to this generalization.

10. Recent studies of American Jews contain information of this sort. See, for example, Lazerwitz and Harrison: Fred Massarik, "Affiliation and Non-Affiliation in the United States Jewish Community: A Reconceptualization," *American Jewish Year Book, 1978* (Philadelphia: Jewish Publication Society, 1978), pp. 262-274; Charles S. Liebman, "Changing Social Characteristics of Orthodox, Conservative and Reform Jews," *Sociological Analysis*, 27 (Winter 1966):210–222.

11. One of the most important of such studies and a model for many others was Gerhard Lenski, *The Religious Factor* (Garden City, N.Y.: Doubleday, 1961), which asked what consequences if any do religious affiliation, belief, and association have for family, economic and political activity and attitudes. Other studies have focused on religion and prejudice, religion and pathological behavior, religion and values, etc. A vast number of empirical studies of religious behavior is summarized in Michael Argyle and Benjamin Beit-Hallahmi, *The Social Psychology of Religion* (London: Routledge and Kegan Paul, 1975).

12. It is difficult to single out any one item in this vast literature. I suppose that three studies deserve special mention. One, which has received a great deal of attention from sociologists of religion and does make some effort at theoretical formulation rather than mere description, is Charles Y. Glock and Robert N. Bellah, eds. *The New Religious Consciousness* (Berkeley: The University of California Press, 1976). The second book describes the origins of the Moonies and was researched before that group had achieved its remarkable success: John Lofland, *Doomsday Cult* (New York: Halstead Press, 1977). The third book deals with the rise of religious conservatism; Dean M. Kelley, *Why Conservative Churches Are Growing* (New York: Harper and Row, 1972), but see also Reginald Bibby, "Why Conservative Churches *Really* Are Growing: Kelley Revisited," *Journal for the Scientific Study of Religion* 17 (June 1978): 129–137.

13. Charles Y. Glock and Phillip E. Hammond, eds. *Beyond the Classics: Essays in the Scientific Study of Religion* (New York: Harper and Row, 1973), p. xiii.

14. This essay was written in 1979 though it wasn't published until 1981. At that time most social scientists were still convinced that religion had declined. I have left this part of my original essay intact because it enables me to develop a point that deserves making regardless of the changed perception of social scientists about the decline or non-decline of religion. In fact, if we measure religion by church membership or belief in God or personal testimony about the importance of religion in one's life, the evidence continues to attest to religious decline in industrial Europe but no decline in the United States. For a number of essays that make this point very dramatically see, *Unsecular America* ed. John Neuhaus (Grand Rapids, Michigan: William Eerdman's Publishing Co., 1986). A strong statement about the inevitability of religious decline in the modern world is Bryan Wilson, *Contemporary Transformations of Religion* (London: Oxford University Press, 1976). The contemporary view offering a theoretical rationale for the strength of religion in the modern world is to be found in *The Sacred in a Secular Age* ed. Phillip Hammond (Berkeley: University of California Press, 1985). The turning point was, probably, the essay by Daniel Bell, "Return of the Sacred? The Argument on the Future of Religion," *British Journal of Sociology* 38 (December 1977):419–449.

15. Greeley is a voluminous writer. The most relevant of his books on this theme is *Unsecular Man* (New York: Schocken Books, 1975).

16. David Hay and Ann Morisy, "Reports of Ecstatic, Paranormal or Religious

Experience in Great Britain and the Untied States - A Comparison of Trends," *Journal for the Scientific Study of Religion* 17 (September 1978):255–268.

17. Alternatively, one may redefine the concept "secular" and argue that if secularization hasn't increased, then religion hasn't declined. For an ingenious treatment see David Martin, *The Religious and The Secular* (New York: Schocken Books, 1969). Finally, one may argue that religion has indeed declined but this signals the decline of civilization or society itself. Wilson makes such an argument.

18. Greeley is also associated with this point of view:

     ... religion is not church attendance, ritual observance, doctrinal code, denominational affiliation, or propositional orthodoxy. Religion is, on the contrary, a human's definition of the Real, an interpretative scheme, a primal culture system, ultimate values, answers to questions of injustice, suffering surprise, life and death.
     William C. McCready with Andrew M. Greeley, *The Ultimate Values of the American Population* (Beverly Hills: Sage, 1976), p. 179.

19. Thomas Luckmann, *The Invisible Religion* (New York: Macmillan, 1967).

20. The discussion relies upon Peter Berger, *The Sacred Canopy* (Garden City, N.Y.: Doubleday, 1969) who shares many of Luckmann's perspectives; Clifford Geertz, *Islam Observed* (New Haven: Yale University Press, 1968), and "Religion As A Cultural System," in Clifford Geertz, *The Interpretation of Cultures* (New York: Basic Books, 1973), pp. 87–125; Robert N. Bellah, *Beyond Belief* (New York: Harper and Row, 1970); and to a lesser extent on Victor Turner and his disciples whose specific contributions are discussed below.

21. Geertz, "The Interpretation . . . ," pp. 93–94.

22. One generally thinks of religious practices in terms of religious rituals or rites which are by definition symbolic. However, there are religious practices such as giving of charity which are neither rituals or rites. Judaism knows many such practices. Secondly, whereas one generally approaches the holy in a ritualized, that is a formalized, manner, this need not necessarily be the case. Both these caveats have been neglected by sociologists of religion. Religious beliefs also need not be symbolic. We can distinguish between cognitive assertions of belief (theology) and mythic assertions. The latter is far more laden with symbol. The former frequently eschews it.

23. An example of a study which does relate religion and organization is Paul M. Harrison's study of the Baptist Church, *Authority and Power in the Free Church Tradition* (Princeton: Princeton University Press, 1959).

24. Victor Turner, *The Ritual Process* (Chicago: Aldine, 1969).

25. Ibid., p. 138.

26. Robert Bocock, *Ritual in Industrial Society* (London: George Allen and Unwin, 1974); Sally Falk Moore and Barbara G. Myerhoff, eds., *Secular Ritual* (Assen/Amsterdam: Van Gorcum, 1977), are of special interest because their treatment of non-religious ritual illuminates the particular meaning and function of sacred and religious ritual.

27. An excellent illustration is Michael H. Ducey, *Sunday Morning: Aspects of Urban Ritual* (New York: The Free Press, 1977).

28. Mary Douglas, *Natural Symbols* (New York: Random House, Vintage, 1973). Douglas' earlier study, *Purity and Danger* (London: Routledge and Kegan Paul,

1966), is also an extremely suggestive work. Jacob Neusner has utilized Douglas' earlier book in his study of the mishnaic code of Purities.

29. Ibid., p. 48.
30. Ibid., pp. 72–73.
31. This is true despite Eliade's own insistence on the importance of myth in contemporary life. On this point, in particular, see Mircea Eliade, "Myths, Dreams and Mysteries: The Encounter between Contemporary Faiths and Archaic Realities," reprinted in *Myth and Symbol*, ed. F.W. Dillistone (London: S.P.C.K., 1966), pp. 35–50. For Eliade's more general treatment of myth see *The Sacred and the Profane* (New York: Harcourt Brace and World, Willard Trask, trans. 1959). On Levi-Strauss' treatment of myth see "The Structured Study of Myth" reprinted in *Reader in Comparative Religion* eds. William Lessa and Evan Vogt (New York: Harper and Row, second ed., 1965), pp. 561–574.
32. There are exceptions. I only mean to contrast the paucity of helpful material on myth with the abundance of material on ritual.
33. The definition by the German theologian Schniewind is cited in Edmund Leach, *Genesis As Myth* (London: Jonathan Cape, 1969), p. 7.
34. I discuss the Holocaust and its relationship to the Jacob-Esau myth in Charles S. Liebman, "Myth, Tradition and Values in Israeli Society," *Midstream,* 24 (January 1978): 44–53. I offer a fuller discussion of the role of myth in contemporary Israeli society in Charles Liebman and Eliezer Don-Yehiya, *Civil Religion in Israel* (Berkeley: University of California Press, 1983).
35. Bellah, pp. 168–189.
36. Ibid., p. 175.
37. Leonard Glick, "The Anthropology of Religion: Malinowski and Beyond," Glock and Hammond, p. 213.
38. Jonathan Woocher, *Sacred Survival* (Bloomington: Indiana University Press, 1986).

3

Religious Extremism

Studies of American Jews challenge the prevailing notions in the social sciences. There are those who have sought to study American Jews from the inside. These authors raise questions that concern the organized Jewish community or that concern individual Jews or that concern the author him/herself as a Jew. While these studies may utilize conceptions prevalent in the social sciences they do not derive from any body of social science theory and contribute very little to those interested in other ethnic or religious groups. The majority of studies written about American Jews are of this type. These are books written by Jews, about Jews, for Jewish audiences. The social scientist, in his role as social scientist reads them with some degree of uneasiness. They may be well written, intelligent, helpful to him in understanding Judaism but they seem peripheral to the discipline of social science.

On the other hand, the few efforts that have been made to produce studies of American Jews that proceed from a theoretical perspective anchored in the social sciences have been most unsatisfactory, at least to me. Sometimes I have the feeling that such authors are describing a reality that has little to do with American Jews. Other times I feel they are stating the obvious.I suspect that the fault lies primarily with social science theory and only secondarily, if at all, with the paucity of gifted students of American Jewish life.

I don't believe that the theoretical instruments available to social scientists are very powerful or very efficacious. Some of them, however, bear a certain glamour or patina that deceives us into believing that they offer accurate tools with which to describe reality. They seem to have a surface credibility. When we apply these theoretical instruments to descriptions of situations about which we know very little, and what we know we know only as outsiders, our confidence in these theories is reinforced. Furthermore, when these theories are taught in graduate schools by distinguished professors to gullible students (gullability may be a necessary quality for

25

completing one's graduate studies) they become confused with reality it-self.They then begin to assume the status of the self-fulfilling theory. We forget that these theories are simply conceptions which may or may not be helpful in describing reality and they become, instead, descriptions which we impose upon reality. It is becoming increasingly obvious that moderni-zation theory in its various permutations is one such illustration. We know today that third-world studies of the fifties and sixties are of limited value because they proceeded from theoretical assumptions which in retrospect appear far fetched. Yet these theories are associated with the great figures of sociology and political science.[1]

The advantage American Jewish studies enjoys is the fact that both authors and readers know too much about the subject from the inside to be deceived by social science theory. The result isn't necessarily better studies but it does mean studies which are spared at least one of the handicaps of other works in the social sciences.

I am not entirely cynical about the value of social science in the study of contemporary Jews. Indeed, as the previous chapter suggests, I think that many concepts in the sociology of religion can be useful when applied to the study of American Judaism. The other side of the coin is that many conceptions of social scientists can be tested against the reality of contem-porary Jewish life; a reality about which enough people are sufficiently well informed so that they will avoid falling prey to the seductive qualities and sometimes elegant formulations of contemporary theory. A good example is the case of "religious extremism."

Judaism, in both Israel and the United States (as well as other parts of the world) is experiencing a rise in religious extremism or at least a per-ceived rise in religious extremism. Since this phenomenon is not peculiar to Judaism the explanation that one offers cannot be peculiar to Judaism. On the other hand, it would be quite remarkable if developments in the belief and behavior patterns of religious adherents, particularly those most zealous in their attachment to the religion, were entirely accounted for by developments extrinsic to the religion. As David Martin notes, the ethos of a church "colors whatever may be the functional logic of its social posi-tion."[2] Hence, the focus on Judaism is not to suggest that this is what happens to every historical religion but rather to raise issues through which other communities can be compared and distinguished.

Why Study Religious Extremism

The rise of religious extremism was not anticipated by modernization theory which dominated the social sciences until a decade ago.[3] The expla-nation that I offer also argues that prevailing paradigms among social scientists lead to the wrong question and a focus on the wrong sorts of information. Even if the explanation I offer is incorrect, this focus on religious extremism draws attention to an important topic for the scientific study of religion.

Extremism, whatever form it takes, is an affirmation of "the more the better." Hence, it is helpful to know what it is that the extremists want "more" of. What elements of religion do different extremist groups focus on? Are they similar from one religion to another? Can the internal structure of the particular religion or of religion in general help account for the particular emphasis? Can we distinguish types of extremist groups within the same religion by the elements they focus on, and are these groups identifiable by standard social characteristics such as age, occupation, income, education, religious background, and so on?

Defining Religious Extremism

Religious extremism can refer to either a process or to an institution. By the term process I mean, for example, referring to an individual or a group which has become more or less religiously extreme. It is commonplace among Orthodox Jews in both Israel and the United States to observe that their children have become more religiously extreme (for example, they resist secular education or are disdainful of western culture). Many non-Orthodox Jews in the United States point to the growing extremism within American Orthodoxy citing, as an example, Orthodox resistance to cooperation with or recognition of Conservative or Reform rabbis. By the term institution I mean, for example, the reference to a particular group or a particular individual identified as extreme so that anything which that group or that individual does automatically becomes the bench mark of extremism. The Satmar *hasidim* (a pietistic group of Jews located in the Williamsberg section of Brooklyn) is considered the most religiously extreme Jewish group. Any study of the Satmar hasidim automatically constitutes a study of religious extremism. To say that there has been a growth of religious extremism can therefore mean that more and more people are behaving in a religiously extreme manner, or that there is an increase in strength and/or influence of groups identified as religiously extreme. The two phenomena may, but need not necessarily, be associated. In theory, strengthening the process of extremism might weaken the attraction of institutional extremism. If a group of religious moderates is now becoming religiously extreme they may be able to compete more effectively with the institutional extremists.

I assume that in most contemporary societies there is a term comparable to or interchangeable with religious extremism, and that the processes or institutions to which it refers are readily identifiable, even if they are not easily definable. The scholar's first task is to define religious extremism in a way that corresponds as closely as possible to that which is popularly identified as religious extremism. The following definition is based on my impression of what Jews in general (but Israeli and American Jews in particular) label as religious extremism and on the characteristics of those groups whom the public identifies as extremist. (The term extremism does carry negative value connotations but no such connotations are intended here. Those more sympathetic to the phenomenon are likely to label it zealousness). I am also trying to identify some essential characteristic of extremism within the category of religion. Hence, I deliberately avoid defining extremism as a relative term. Obviously, along any range of opinion or behavior the set at one or the other end of the continuum is going to be "extreme." In this respect, one can identify extremists among every religious group no matter how moderate its orientation. One can talk about Unitarian and Bahai extremists, or, among Jews, Conservative or Reform extremists . That is not what I have in mind. In the context of this chapter, Jewish religious extremism is located within the world of Orthodox Judaism. I suggest that there are three dimensions to religious extremism. The first contains three components.

Expansion of Religious Law

The first dimension of Jewish religious extremism is the effort to expand *halakhah* (religious law). Religious law is the set of rules Jews are obliged to obey lest they sin against God. The sin many be a violation of one's responsibility to God or to other persons. Its sanction may be a matter of human and/or divine judgement. This is irrelevant for purposes of definition. Judaism, like Islam, is defined and distinguished from other religions and cultures by its particular code of law. Because of the prime importance of the law, it stands to reason that Jewish religious extremists will express their orientations, at least in part, in their conception of *halakhah*. Perhaps this is less true among Christians or Buddhists among whom religious law plays a smaller role. On the other hand, perhaps law, by its nature, (objective, clear cut, authoritative) is an especially attractive focus for extremists of all religious traditions. This question merits further study.

An extremist orientation to *halakhah* has three components. First, extremists seek to expand its scope. One can conceive of a continuum of activity from the collective to the private in which religious law is relevant. At one end of the continuum would be collective behavior, for example, the political or economic structure of society as expressed in public law. Further along the continuum are aspects of public law which are concerned with private as opposed to collective behavior. Family law is "the last bastion of the religious concept of law" in the sense of public law imposed on all citizens.[4] But the continuum of religious concern extends further. After all, religion is also concerned with the realm of private behavior which needn't necessarily find expression in public law. It is hard to conceive of a religion prepared to admit that it has nothing authoritative to say to its adherents about education or sex even if that religion eschews enactment of its injunctions in public law. The issue which most religions face is not whether abortion is or is not a sin, not whether pre-marital intercourse is immoral, not whether homosexuality is an abomination in the eyes of God, but whether they ought to impose their religious conceptions upon the public in the form of secular law. Extremists are at this end of the continuum. They seek to extend the scope of religious law to include the public as well as the private realm and to matters of collective as well as private behavior within that realm.

Expanding the scope of *halakhah* also means that Jewish extremists have a social program and are critical of existing social institutions, though different groups of extremists may each have their own program. Extremists may seek to impose their program on society in the immediate present, thereby necessarily involving themselves in political conflict, or they may withdraw from society, awaiting a more propitious time, perhaps Divine intervention, for the realization of their program. In the latter case, political conflict may be limited to the defense of the extremists' autonomy. The conquest tendency as opposed to the withdrawal tendency may be a function of a realistic assessment of the political environment and/or a function of the group's ideology. Of course, in some cases neither option may be feasible, as Ivan Marcus notes in his study of a medieval extremist Jewish group, in which case the extremists live *in* but not *of* the world.[5]

The second component of the extremists' orientation to *halakhah* is in the elaboration of the details of the law. For example, religious law requires modesty of dress, particularly among women. The question is: does the *halakhah* require "modesty" and allow each individual or each community to decide on its application? Or, as extremists aver, is the law detailed, requiring, for example, sleeves or hemlines of a certain length?

The first two components in the extremists' orientation to *halakhah* share a common characteristic. They emphasize the objective, the ordained, and they limit the authority of the subjective, the optional, of personal interpretation. They do not, however, minimize the importance of inward motivation. This is of no less importance to extremists than to religious moderates.

The third component in the expansion of the law is the question of strictness versus leniency in interpretation. The law, even if detailed, might be lenient (for example, requiring sleeves to the elbow and hemlines to just below the knees) or it might be strict (requiring that all parts of the body be covered). The term strict does not necessarily mean closer to the "letter of the law." The "letter of the law" often points to a lenient interpretation. Strict refers to the imposition of greater restriction and hardships which is what extremists welcome.[6]

Social Isolation

The second dimension of religious extremism is its attitude toward those elements of society who do not accept extremist norms. The characteristic approach of extremism is one of isolation. However, when coupled with efforts to convert or persuade other individuals, the isolation is tempered and special safeguards may be erected to mitigate the dangers which the inevitable contact with outsiders invites. This is true, for example, of the followers of the ḥasidic group called *Ḥabad* better known as the Lubavitcher ḥasidim, or adherents of the Lubavitcher *rebbe*.[7] The purer form of social isolation, though also not total, is found among Israeli Jews who are part of the *Edah Ḥaredit* (Community of the Pious) centered in Jerusalem with a secondary center in B'nei B'rak.[8] In the United States, Jewish extremists have isolated themselves in neighborhoods of New York City and its suburbs. But the isolated neighborhood is not absolutely critical to Jewish extremists nor is it feasible given the structure of the modern city. A strong measure of social isolation can, however, be maintained even under conditions of mixed neighborhoods. Needless to say, Jewish extremists who seek to maximize social isolation are less threatened by the mixtures of the occupants of the neighborhoods in which many of them do live (for example, Blacks and Hispanics), than they would be by the presence of Conservative or Reform Jews.

Judaism is probably the most ethnically oriented of all historical religions. Whereas isolation from non-Jews is encouraged, distancing oneself from other Jews is a problem. It has only become *halakhically* normative in the modern era.[9] In fact, I suspect that one difference between groups of modern and pre-modern Jewish extremists is that the latter had to develop a distinctive program and elaborate world view to legitimate their isolation from and/or hostility toward the Jewish community. In this respect, extremist groups in the pre-modern period tended to be sects. Sects and cults are definable by a distinctive world view or meaning system in addition to an independent organizational structure. In the modern period, the rise of extremism as a process, for reasons to be discussed later, has legitimated isolation. This is, in fact, the strategy Orthodox Jews as a group adopt in their relationships with non-Orthodox Jews. Extremist groups within the religious world no longer seek elaborate legitimation for their position. Non-sect-like religious extremism may, therefore, be a particularly modern phenomenon among Jews. Thus, an extremist group is not necessarily sectarian nor are sects necessarily extremists. Extremists don't necessarily have a world view or meaning system which distinguishes them from the majority of Orthodox Jews, although they are likely to give greater emphasis to one aspect or another of the prevailing world view or meaning system. Over the long run, extremists may become sectarians developing a world view which elaborates their own interpretation of the religion, protects them against hostile outsiders, and explains their condition, but this is less likely in our time precisely because there is no organized community of outsiders other than that which the extremists create in their own minds.

Cultural Rejection

The third dimension of religious extremism is the rejection of cultural forms and values that are not perceived as indigenous to the religious tradition. Such a position is difficult to maintain for any but the strictest sects. Pursuing such a goal with consistency would mean the creation of alternate channels for cultural transmission (publishing houses, newspapers, radio, television stations). Even if the group is small and intimate enough to forgo such channels, it must still prohibit exposure to the media in the hands of outsiders. There are Jewish extremists who successfully do so. Extremists, in both Israel and the United States have their own publishing houses (some of their children's books are of such fine quality that sales extend to non-extremists as well) and their own quasi-newspapers. They cope with the problem of television by forbidding its use. Other groups may be less prepared to adopt a public stance of hostility toward the media or more anxious to use the media to convince the non-Orthodox of their cause. One way in which they protect their own adherents from outside influence (this is particularly true of *Ḥabad*) is by so occupying them with all kinds of activity that there is little leisure time for exposure to the mass media.(Study of sacred text is one example but the Lubavitcher leaders who cater to a non-intellectually elitist community devise all kinds of projects requiring great investments of time and energy.)

The Limits of Religious Extremism

Religious extremism, as defined here, is destructive of any communal structure. The obvious question is whether extremism doesn't destroy itself in the long run. The answer is that it would if it could exist in pure form. Extremism is "pure" religion in the sense of being totally differentiated from other forms of culture and independent of all social institutions. That is why it might best be described as an ideal typical impulse rather than as objectified in individuals or institutions. All historical religions recognized the destructive capacity of extremism and sought strategies to contain it. In fact, I believe that Jewish extremism is on the rise because the breakdown of the Jewish community has weakened its capacity to check extremist impulses. But once extremism or extremists organize to attain their goals, the process of organization introduces the very communal-type constraint from which extremism initially freed itself. Extremism cannot exist in reality. Metaphorically, it might be said that extremism searches for freedom from communal constraints and the instant it succeeds it begins to restrain *itself* in order to achieve the very purposes for which it sought its freedom. The problem merits more rigorous empirical examination which can draw on the church-sect literature and other case studies among Jews as well as non-Jews.[10]

Explaining Religious Moderation

The central argument presented here is that a propensity to religious extremism does not require explanation since it is entirely consistent with basic religious tenets and authentic religious orientations. It is religious moderation or religious liberalism, the willingness of religious adherents to accommodate themselves to their environment, to adapt their behavioral and belief pattern to prevailing cultural norms, to make peace with the world, that requires explanation. As suggested, however, objectifying extremism in persons or institutions, distinguishing extremists from non-extremists, leaves the misleading impression that there is a pure form of extremism in reality. If my description of the extremist orientation is correct, then extremism is a tendency to which every religiously oriented person is attracted. What are some factors of major importance which have mitigated the natural propensity of religion toward extremism?

The most obvious factor is the historical association of religion, culture, and society. Religious institutions arise within a specific culture and society. Religious extremism assumes a very high level of religious differentiation. Extremism is restrained when religion is an organic part of the society diffused throughout its institutions. Where differentiation has taken place, the religious institution is often impelled to worldly activity in order to maximize its autonomy, control its environment, protect itself, attract adherents, and so on. The need for the approval of others and the interaction with other economic and political institutions introduces a compromising or adaptationist tendency.

Furthermore, the success of religion confers status and material benefits on its leaders and attracts to its ranks individuals with self interested motivation, orientations and propensities.[11]

Finally, religion is not unidimensional. It not only finds room for but may even cultivate qualities and orientations such as contemplation, study, quietude, passivity or the search for a sense of peace, which are inconsistent with extremist orientations.

If, at the present time, we are witnessing a rise in religious extremism, the explanation must lie in a weakening of the very forces that negated extremism in the past. My concern is with contemporary Judaism, but to understand the rise of extremism today one must begin with the condition of Jewish Orthodoxy in the modern period.

The Rise of Modern Jewish Extremism

The watershed period for all of modern Judaism is associated with Jewish enlightenment and the movement for political emancipation.[12] This begins in central and western Europe in the middle of the late eighteenth century, extends to eastern Europe by the middle of the nineteenth century and begins penetrating the Jewish communities in Muslim lands at the end of the last and beginning of the present century.[13]

The enlightenment and emancipation were distinctive movements whose combined impact destroyed traditional modes of religious thought and behavior at the individual level, and the capacity of the Jewish community to enforce its regulations at the communal level. The outcome meant the differentiation of religious and secular authority, the diminished capacity of all Jewish leaders to impose their injunctions upon individual Jews, and the diminished legitimacy of community-wide authorities. One consequence was the destruction of the most important force mitigating religious extremism: communal unity. Communal unity was not only a religious value but a necessity for Jews as protection against a hostile environment. It was facilitated by the medieval world which required Jews to organize themselves in independent corporate communities which mediated the relationships between the individual Jew and the non-Jewish authorities. The corporate Jewish community, its leaders in particular, were sensitive to the threat which extremism evoked, however legitimate that extremism might have been in religious terms. It would be most instructive if we had more studies of how the community dealt with extremism prior to the emancipation period. Apparently, it utilized techniques of cooptation as well as excommunication. But it could not leave extremism unchecked lest it generate a momentum that would destroy the community.

In the pre-emancipation period, extremist tendencies or inclinations were probably present among many, if not most, Jews—rabbinical leaders in particular. But these tendencies were in tension with, and held in check by a sense of responsibility for the material and physical welfare of the entire community, and by the network of interrelationships between more religious and less religious Jews as well as between Jews and non-Jews. This last point may appear paradoxical. After all, the enlightenment and emancipation presumably permitted Jews much freer contact with non-Jews. While that is true, these contacts occurred in a relatively religiously neutral context. To borrow an application from role theory in the social sciences, the contacts in the new period, did not ostensibly occur between Jew and non-Jew but between two persons engaged in business, or between merchant and customer or doctor and patient, one of whom *happened* to be a Jew and one of whom *happened* to be a non-Jew. As the fact of one's Jewishness became less and less relevant in the contact between Jews and non-Jews, the interrelationship itself, at least in some respects, became less Jewishly relevant. It therefore freed the extremist from responsibility for the consequences of his behavior on interrelationships between groups of Jews or between Jews and non-Jews. The pre-modern period is hardly cut of one cloth but if we compare Orthodox Jews and their leaders in the pre-emancipation period with those of today then most contemporary religious Jews are more extreme (according to the definition of extremism offered here) than were their predecessors. In light of the above, this is not surprising.

The major battlefront around which extremism formed itself was its rejection of the enlightenment and the emancipation; more properly a rejection of the enlightenment because of its intrinsic qualities and a rejection of the emancipation because of its consequences. A convenient label for both is "modernity" although not all the features of "modernity" were immediately apparent. Jacob Katz has observed that traditional religious leaders were alarmed by the accumulation and severity of deviations from Jewish law and the claim of "the transgressors that they were acting from conviction and therefore had the right to go their own ways."[14] The claim that acting from conviction affords one the right to dictate the nature of one's spiritual life evokes Peter Berger's definition of modern consciousness as "the movement from fate to choice."[15]

Those Jews who rejected modernity or its consequences now had to develop institutions and structures to insulate the tradition from the new environment. The affirmationists, on the other hand, were those who remained committed to the religious tradition but welcomed or made accommodations to the opportunities afforded by the modern age even if they were conscious of its dangers. Both affirmationists and rejectionists, to borrow a term Peter Berger has applied to Christianity's confrontation with modernity, were religious innovators.[16] The rise of extremism is the story of the rise of the rejectionist and decline of the affirmationist orientation.

Was affirmationism an authentic religious response? It depends on how one understands the term "authentic." Affirmationism can be partially accounted for by self-interested motivations of religious leaders and adherents to whom religion continued to provide respectability and status well into the twentieth century. An important factor was the sense of overwhelming power and attractiveness which modern culture had for many Jews, particularly in western Europe. Rabbinical leaders there often spoke of the futility of opposing modernity. It is as if they were reconciled to affirmationism as a strategy for survival. But many of the same leaders were themselves attracted by aspects of contemporary culture. The great rabbinic authority who sang German operas after his Sabbath meal[17] was not reconciling himself to modern culture for instrumental purposes. But there were also those who viewed the political and social changes wrought by the emancipation as the "beginning of the Redemption" and a sign that humanity (meaning Jews) was capable, by its own effort, of undertaking the tasks that would culminate in the coming of the Messiah. At one point the rejectionists were forced to argue less against the emancipation itself than against the notion that it had created a novel condition in Jewish life when things had never been so good.[18] The affirmationists argued that the marked and dramatic improvement in the Jewish condition could only be a sign of God's favor and the beginning of a new era which also legitimated a new world view. This led the rejectionists to argue that improvements in the Jewish condition were not necessarily novel and, therefore, did not signal the beginning of a new era. While the affirmationists may have had reservations and doubts about their own ability to withstand the forces of modernity, they never doubted that they were in closer touch with the forces of the future than were the rejectionists.

The Decline of Religious Moderation

What forces weakened the affirmationists and strengthened the rejectionists? I already suggested one reason. In addition, economic prosperity had opposite effects on each group. Among the former, prosperity and increased secular education resulted in religious laxity, the adoption of more liberal religious beliefs, a rejection of ritual and the substitution of ethical conceptions of religion comparable to those found among the non-Jewish population.[19] But the rejectionists eschewed secular education, so its impact was reduced. Economic prosperity strengthened their independence and facilitated their isolation or insulation from the social and cultural environment.[20] Economic prosperity, for example, permitted the establishment of an elaborate educational network providing intense socialization to rejectionist values. Increased wealth has meant that children (sons in particular) can be maintained in such institutions into their late twenties, a point to which I return in the next chapter. In Israel, major support for these institutions comes from the government, a function of both the political influence of the religious sector but also of a level of national prosperity which permits the maintenance of such institutions by the public sector. In the United States support comes primarily from private donors. Not all these donors are themselves part of the rejectionist camp, indeed many are not even Orthodox. This is a point to which I will also return in the next chapter. Among the donors who are rejectionists some are of relatively little means who, like many of the contributors to Christian and Moslem fundamentalist causes, see in such contributions both the hope of realizing a social or political ideal and the fulfillment of a basic religious command. In other words, these forms of philanthropy are inherently virtuous.But most of the support from rejectionist donors to these institutions comes from a number of exceedingly wealthy individuals who have built their own businesses and prospered mightily since the end of the 1940s. This is an important factor in accounting for the relatively recent strength of the rejectionist camp among Orthodox Jews.

The breakdown of the corporate Jewish community, the *kehilla*[21] and the substitution of a voluntaristic pluralistic community has meant that rejectionists are no longer accountable to more moderate elements. The path is now open to the creation of independent rejectionist institutions. The consequences of voluntarism and pluralism are not pronounced among the religious elite, among whom one would expect to find the strongest propensity to extremism because they are more religiously committed than the non-elite and because the kind of education required to become a master of religious law socializes them to a rejectionist point of view. In addition, the general decline of the status and role of religious institutions in the society means that people are less attracted to religion for self-interested purposes. Hence, the more worldly, more accommodationist, less principled type of individual who might have once sought a position of religious leadership now looks elsewhere to satisfy his ambitions.

In the past, rabbinical authorities, responsible for the entire community, were reluctant to interpret religious law in such a manner that the vast majority of Jews would find its observance excessively burdensome. *Halakhic* authorities have been relieved of this constraint by their sense that the vast majority wouldn't observe Jewish law regardless of how they interpreted it. On the other hand, the Orthodox minority are ready to accept almost any ruling of their *halakhic* authorities. There are a few exceptions and they demonstrate the rule. An outstanding example is the unwillingness of most *halakhic* authorities to forbid cigarette smoking although its menace to life clearly places it within the category of prohibited acts. This is one of the few injunctions, however, which cigarette smokers among the Orthodox are likely to violate.

The voluntarism and pluralism of the community exposes the affirmationists to the influence of non-Orthodox and even non-Jewish conceptions of appropriate religious belief and behavior. No better example exists than notions about the appropriate role and status of women; notions that the affirmationists have absorbed from the non-Orthodox and non-Jewish environment but which have penetrated the rejectionist world to a very slight degree and in some instances (e.g. forbidding women to pray in independent groups), has even engendered a backlash of rejectionism. Religion, built on principles of eternity and inerrancy has difficulty absorbing the rapid changes which characterise modernity. The rejectionists are not only unaffected but perhaps are even strengthened by the contrast between their own seemingly uninterrupted, unchanging culture and that which surrounds them. The affirmationists, on the other hand, face the dilemma of reconciling their religious conceptions with this self-consciously changing culture.

Ideological factors also operate to the benefit of the rejectionists and the disadvantage of affirmationists. Among Orthodox Jews, there are different types of affirmationist responses some of which I discuss in the next chapter. But none of them enjoy widespread rabbinical sanction. Religious commitment, in the context of the Jewish tradition and certainly for the Orthodox Jew today, as I indicated at the outset of this chapter, means first and foremost, a commitment to the observance of Jewish law as it is interpreted by leading rabbinic authorities whose own credentials rest on their mastery and knowledge of the law. The legitimacy of the affirmationists is not only undermined by the paucity of masters of law in their camp, but also by the presence among them of some erstwhile Orthodox Jews who seek legitimacy for or at least behave with indifference to elements of *halakhah*. I discuss this group in the following chapter where I call them "adaptationists." Here I am only concerned with noting that the presence of the adaptationists and the absence of rabbinic scholars undermines the motives of the whole affirmationist camp and makes the rejectionists appear more devout in the eyes of the affirmationists themselves.

What I have said in the last three paragraphs must appear strange to someone removed from devoutly religious circles. I will restate it in somewhat different terms. Whereas rejectionists legitimate themselves by Orthodoxy's own criteria of what is Jewishly proper, the affirmationists have recourse to legitimation outside the *halakhic* framework. They may legitimate their position in terms of accommodating to their environment, by admitting to human weakness, in terms of universalist ethical concerns, or even in terms of Jewish philosophical and theological conceptions; but they have difficulty legitimating themselves in terms that all Orthodox Jews acknowledge as primary to Judaism—Jewish law. They cannot do this, in part, because they tend to be more lax in their own observance of Jewish law than is true of the rejectionists and in part because they cannot find *halakhic* authorities who will publicly defend their permissiveness even when it falls within the framework of the permissable.

I will illustrate this point with a personal observation about the use of elevators on the Sabbath in New York. Orthodox Jews believe that pressing an elevator button on the Sabbath is prohibited because it involves "turning on" electricity, an act that all *halakhic* authorities agree is prohibited. However, *halakhic* authorities disagree as to the source of this prohibition and therein lies a very important consideration. Some believe that the prohibition of turning on electricity derives directly from the Biblical prohibition of kindling a fire on the Sabbath. Others, however, believe that one is forbidden to turn on electricity on the Sabbath because the rabbis, in an extension of the Biblical prohibition of kindling fire, decided to forbid it. The consequences of whether turning on electricity is prohibited by Biblical or rabbinic law are very significant. Rabbinic law also prohibits asking a non-Jew to perform an act that is prohibited on the Sabbath if it is for the sole convenience of the individual Jew rather than for the Jewish community. But this prohibition applies to acts that are biblically rather than rabbinically proscribed. I know a number of Orthodox Jews living in high-rise apartment buildings in New York City who have arranged with their doormen (non-Jews) to press the elevator button for them when they enter their buildings on the Sabbath. This, in their opinion is permissable since turning on electricity on the Sabbath is a rabbinic rather than a Biblical prohibition, and therefore, there is no objection to asking a non-Jew to perform this rabbinically prohibited act. But most Orthodox Jews I know who have an elevator button pressed for them are rather uncomfortable about it. The fact that some of them are rabbis and are convinced that the prohibition of turning on electricity is indeed rabbinic rather than biblical in origin makes no difference to them. They think of their behavior as a concession to their own weakness (physical and spiritual) and they are proud of rather than embarrassed by their own children who walk up the stairs rather than use the elevator.

I don't want to suggest that the sole distinction between affirmationists and rejectionists is in the former's more permissive attitude toward *halakhah*. In the past, and to some extent today, basic issues of ethical sensitivity and intellectual conceptions divided them. At one point in time it appeared that class differences explained propensities to one or the other position but this appears less and less to be the case. To the extent that one can speak of an affirmationist conception (and as I have suggested, there are a number of affirmationist positions) distinct from a rejectionist conception (rejectionists are also divided among themselves on a number of issues) it is fair to say that the affirmationists never affirmed their position as *the* correct position and the rejectionist position as an incorrect one. The most they claimed for themselves was a parity of legitimacy. (The one exception to this rule was the claim by the religious zionists that on the issue of zionism they were correct and the rejectionists incorrect. The fact that such claims are increasingly muted in recent years is further evidence of the rise of the extremist position.) The rejectionists, on the other hand, never accorded the same legitimacy to the affirmationists. The affirmationists were further weakened, as we have noted, by the sense of many, particularly among the younger generation, that affirmationism was not an ideology but a facade for *halakhic* deviation.

If one is not looking for a strategy to affirm modern culture and values, affirmationist conceptions can appear very convincing. If, therefore, the rejectionist position has gained influence in recent years, reasons may also be sought in the declining attractiveness of modern culture and civilization. Indeed, the decline of modernist confidence, the loss of direction characteristic of contemporary western culture, and the decline in ideological certainty has resulted in a decline in that religious orientation which affirmed the value, or at least the inevitable triumph of modern culture. This has special significance in Israel and by extension to Orthodox Jews throughout the world who follow developments in Israeli life rather closely. Secular zionism, the world view that provided the ideological and symbolic foundation for the state of Israel, its identity, legitimacy, and its relationship to world Jewry and the Judaic tradition has lost resonance.[22] The decline of zionism in Israel itself has meant the decline of a system of meaning through which the vast majority of those Jews found answers to basic questions of collective existence and through which many also found personal and private meaning. In terms of our topic, it means that Orthodox Jews raised in affirmationist homes were no longer attracted by a secular ideology that competed with rejectionism as a meaning system. Affirmationism, in its various guises, was an effort to find some compromise between the rejectionist conception of Judaism and the appeal of modern culture and Jewish nationalism. The decline in the attractiveness of both modern culture and Jewish nationalism has strengthened the appeal of rejectionism.

Conclusion

The phenomenon identified as religious extremism is best accounted for by the decline in influence of those factors which led to religious moderation in the past. A characteristic feature of religion is the overriding commitment which it evokes. Indeed, the fact that religion has this meaning in popular usage (e.g., "it's like a religion to him" or "she does it religiously") suggests just this association. Such commitment reflects and supports an extremist orientation in three ways.

First, religion claims to possess absolute truth. It knows the route one must follow to live one's life in accordance with that which is ultimately right and ultimately just. Hence, it is reasonable to expect that religious adherents will welcome the extension of the scope and detail of religious injunctions. This heightens their confidence that everything they and the society of which they are part does, is in accord with the right way. The search for stricter or harsher interpretation of the law is consistent with a desire to assure oneself and others that one is indeed living in accordance with what one is commanded to do rather than simply in accordance with what one would like to do.

Second, whether understood in symbolic or normative terms, culture can be evaluated in terms of religious truth. The injunction to distance oneself from all forms of culture which are not consistent with religious truth is entirely explicable within the framework of religious assumptions, just as religious knowledge is a standard by which one can judge and measure other forms of knowledge and other forms of truth.

Third, since religious commitment is a total commitment, and the behavior it elicits is by definition moral behavior, religious adherence becomes a criteria by which other people can be evaluated. The religiously committed individual will experience moral repugnance in associating with non-religious people. Also, other things being equal, religious commitment leads one to social isolation in order to protect oneself from the influences (accidental or intended) of others, an orientation that may itself be incorporated into the religious framework of injunctions.

In short, religious commitment leads to the three characteristics which define religious extremism. I don't mean to argue that other implications cannot be derived from religious commitment or that true religious belief and practice invariably lead to extremism. I do argue, however, that extremism is an understandable and, other things being equal, the most obvious consequence of religious commitment.

Notes

1. For a discussion of this problem as applied to third world studies with a critique that may even be unduly harsh see Fred R. von der Mehden, *Religion and Modernization in Southeast Asia* (Syracuse: Syracuse University Press, 1986).
2. David Martin, *A General Theory of Secularization* (Oxford: Basil Blackwell, 1978), p.24.

3. See, for example, Lucy Creevey, "Religion and Modernization in Senegal," in *Islam and Political Development* ed. John Esposito (Syracuse: Syracuse University Press, 1980), pp. 207–222 and the literature cited therein.

4. Donald Smith, *Religion and Political Development* (Boston: Little, Brown, 1970), p. 3.

5. Ivan Marcus, *Piety and Society* (Lieden: E.J.Brill, 1980).

6. For an analogous example drawn from the contemporary Moslem experience see John Williams, "Veiling in Egypt as a Political and Social Phenomenon," in *Islam and Development*, ed. John Esposito (Syracuse:Syracuse University Press, 1980), pp. 71–86.

7. There is a surprisingly small sociological-anthropological literature on *Habad* considering their size and influence in contemporary Judaism. Of particular relevance is William Shaffir, "Witnessing as Identity Consolidation: The Case of the Lubavitcher Chassidim," in *Identity and Religion* ed. Hans Mol (Beverly Hills, California: Sage, 1978).

8. Menachem Friedman, "Haredim Confront the Modern City," in *Studies in Contemporary Jewry* II ed. Peter Medding (Bloomington: Indiana University Press, 1986), pp. 74–96.

9. Charles Liebman, "Orthodoxy in American Jewish Life," in *American Jewish Year Book 1965* (Philadelphia: Jewish Publication Society, 1965), pp. 21–98 and see especially pp. 38–40.

10. On church-sect theory the classic source is Ernst Troeltsch, *Social Teachings of the Christian Churches*, 2 vols. (Chicago: University of Chicago Press, 1931. See also, Bryon Wilson, *Magic and the Millennium* (New York: Harper and Row, 1973) and Michael Hill, *A Sociology of Religion* (London: Heinemann, 1973) for a good summary of the literature. The recent outpouring of books and articles on sects and cults is worth exploring for helpful examples.

11. Thomas O'Dea, "Five Dilemmas in the Institutionalization of Religion," *Journal for the Scientific Study of Religion* 1 (Fall 1961):30–39.

12. Jacob Katz, *Out of the Ghetto: The Social Background of Jewish Emancipation 1770–1870* (Cambridge, Mass.: Harvard University Press, 1973).

13. Shlomo Deshen, "The Judaism of Middle Eastern Immigrants," *The Jerusalem Quarterly* no. 13 (Fall 1979):89–110.

14. Katz, p. 146.

15. Peter Berger, *The Heretical Imperative* (Garden City, N.Y.: Doubleday, Anchor Books, 1979), p. 11.

16. Peter Berger, *The Sacred Canopy* (Garden City, N.Y.: Doubleday, Anchor Books, 1969), p. 156.

17. David Ellenson, "Rabbi Esriel Hildesheimer and the Quest for Religious Authority," *Modern Judaism* 1 (September 1981):295.

18. Yosef Salmon, "The Response of the Jewish Public to the Society for the Settlement of Eretz Israel," in *Sefer Shraga* eds. Mordecai Eliav and Yitzhak Rafael (Jerusalem: Mossad Harav Kook, in Hebrew 1981), pp. 15–39.

19. Michael Argyle and Benjamin Beit-Hallahmi, *The Social Psychology of Religion* (London: Routledge and Kegan Paul, 1975), pp. 162–166 and Mary Douglas, *Natural Symbols* (New York: Random House, Vintage Books, 1973).

20. Charles Liebman, "Changing Social Characteristics of Orthodox, Conservative and Reform Jews," *Sociological Analysis* 27 (Winter 1966):210–222; Egon Mayer, *From Suburb to Shtetl: The Jews of Boro Park* (Philadelphia: Temple University Press, 1979).

21. Daniel Elazar, "The Kehilla: From Its Beginning to the End of the Modern Epoch,"in *Public Life in Israel and the Diaspora* eds. Sam Lehman-Wilzig and Bernard Susser (Ramat-Gan, Israel: Bar-Ilan University Press, 1981), pp. 26–63.
22. Charles Liebman and Eliezer Don-Yehiya, *Civil Religion in Israel* (Berkeley: University of California Press, 1983).

4

Orthodoxy Faces Modernity

The subject of Orthodox Judaism and modernity may be treated from a number of perspectives. Historians of modern Judaism have a great deal to say about it; students of Jewish intellectual thought or modern Jewish philosophy have contributed to our understanding of the topic from their point of view. Last but not least, a *talmid hakham*, a master of rabbinic text, operating from within a traditional Jewish world view could provide important insights if challenged to elaborate his view of modernity. This essay, however, reflects the impressions and ruminations of a social scientist. It is appropriate, therefore, to begin with an observation about social science and the study of religion.

The success of Orthodox Judaism (the fact that its membership is no longer declining) is matched and even exceeded by that of other fundamentalist movements in other religions in the United States, Israel, and various other parts of the globe. I use the term "fundamentalism" advisedly. In some respects I think it is an appropriate label for Orthodox Judaism in contrast to non-Orthodox Judaism, and I also believe that Orthodox Jews and Christian fundamentalists share a common agenda of concerns, at least in the United States. In some respects, however, indeed in its technical sense, the term is inappropriate. I am going to digress from my main topic, therefore, and first indicate in what respect I think the term "fundamentalism" is inappropriate when applied to Orthodox Judaism. The digression is worth making because it will help explain the nature of Orthodox Judaism.

The term "fundamentalism" arose in association with American Protestantism. It recalls the twelve volume work titled *The Fundamentals* published between 1910 and 1915.[1] In one important respect fundamentalism remains a uniquely Protestant phenomenon, a phenomenon peculiar to a religious group that lacks an elaborate tradition. The fundamentalists asserted that they could summarize the basic religious propositions of Christianity in a series of fundamental propositions such as the inerrancy of

Scripture. Those who assented to these propositions were properly religious and those who did not assent to them were not. Such a notion can only arise in the absence of religious tradition. Protestantism, unlike Catholicism or Judaism or Islam, lacks a central religious tradition, a history, a set of rituals and ceremonials, a rich and distinctive mythology. It is not a culture. Protestant denominations have traditions but if one is to identify Protestantism as distinct from Catholicism one has to narrow the diversity of denominational traditions. That has been the impact of American revivalism as well. Watching the evangelical preachers on television one is struck by the fact that, religiously speaking, it is only the Bible that they share in common. Religious traditions, because they are cultures, ways of life, interrelationships of belief, historical experience, ceremonials, customs and behavior don't lend themselves to the kind of summary statements associated with fundamentalism.

There are two additional though related reasons that fundamentalism is a peculiarly Protestant phenomenon. Protestants believe that sacred scripture can be properly comprehended by everyone. They believe that the implications of sacred text, whether it be for understanding God and/or for ascertaining appropriate human behavior, can be inferred without the mediation of the tradition and of traditional (i.e., authoritative) commentators. This belief itself erodes the development of tradition by suggesting that one's own interpretation or anyone's contemporary interpretation is as valid as that of past generations.

Judaism and Islam also believe in the inerrancy of their sacred scripture. But their internal debate centers on the meaning or interpretation of scripture. And since it is this debate within their own traditions to which they are heirs, the dogma of inerrancy becomes almost secondary. The dogma lies behind the central question of the meaning of text but it can be assumed rather than pushed to the limelight. It would never dawn on the religiously serious Jew or Muslim to affirm that his/her own unmediated interpretation of the meaning of the text is authoritative. Indeed, the very possibility of unmediated interpretation is dubious for one who has been socialized by a religious tradition. The modern Bible scholar, for example, if he is also a religiously serious person and was raised within a religious tradition must strive mightily to free himself of his own tradition if he is to examine the text with fresh eyes. But this disciplinary exercise, while necessary for modern scholarship, is irrelevant in using the sacred text as a guide to religious belief and behavior. The religiously important debate is over "commentary" to the text, so the inerrancy doctrine need never arise. By contrast, if as in the Protestant conception, one's own reading of the text is of religious consequence, it is of utmost importance to decide whether it is God speaking to one through that text.

Consequently, it is somewhat misleading to assign the term "fundamentalist" to any current movement in Judaism, least of all to that group which the American media labels "ultra-Orthodox." On the other hand, the term fundamentalism has assumed new meanings in current discussion. It has been divorced from its historical Protestant association and commonly refers to a movement or group for whom religion, religious beliefs and values are both ultimate and exclusive. For the fundamentalist, God's revelation, whether directly, through scripture, or through authoritative traditions of scriptural interpretation expresses in clear and simple terms how the individual and society ought to behave and what one ought to believe. Religion, for the fundamentalist, ought to comprise the sole content of culture, the foundation of human association, the blueprint for political goals. In this respect one can talk about Jewish fundamentalism. As I indicate below, not all Orthodox Jews are fundamentalists, even in this popular meaning of the term, but Orthodoxy, taken as a whole, fits the definition.

In no case was the success of fundamentalist groups, Jewish or non-Jewish, anticipated by social scientists. On the contrary, the revival of rigorous religious belief and practice has challenged reigning notions of "modernity" prevalent until the last decade. Virtually all social scientists previously accepted the notion that "modernity," defined as a package of technological development, urbanization, increased wealth and leisure time, social mobility, greater education and mass communication, is accompanied by the secularization of world views and the decline of religious faith and practice. Even today, most social scientists (and I include myself in this category) believe that Weberian notions of secularization, (the "disenchantment" of the world, to borrow Weber's felicitous term) are basically correct. But the evidence around us now dictates important modifications. As a leading student of American Protestantism recently said:

> moderns are not consistent, not on course, in respect to the pure secularization trajectory. Who will successfully name a hypothesis that does justice to our religio-secular, our secular-religious times, people and movement?[2]

Modernity's challenge to religion has been stated most succinctly by Peter Berger in a number of books. Perhaps special mention should be made of *The Heretical Imperative*[3] because, as I was recently told, it circulated among the back-bench occupants of Rabbi Soloveitchik's *shiurim* (lectures) at Yeshiva University for a few years following its publication.

Berger restated his conception of modernity in a recent magazine article co-authored with his wife Brigitte. The challenge of modernity, the Bergers said, is not the telephone, the computer or bypass surgery:

> The issue rather is in the area of modern consciousness, and specifically the experience of relativity, the awareness that all world views and value systems are contingent upon specific historical and social circumstances. . . . The experience of relativity, however, makes it difficult to hold beliefs in the taken-for-granted untroubled way that has always been characteristic of tradition. The individual who has passed through the experience may hold very firm beliefs, but he will be conscious of the fact that he has chosen them. The traditionalist holds his beliefs as givens. Modernization, at its very core, is a movement from destiny to choice. To be modern, however critically, means to assent to this movement.[4]

There is an intellectually compelling quality to this definition of modernity, though I admit that I have mixed feelings about it. On the one hand, it seems to fit the condition of Orthodox Jews in many respects. Unlike Jews of the past, Orthodox Jews today are conscious of having *chosen* to be Orthodox. They are aware of alternative expressions of Judaism. Indeed, the distinguishing feature of present-day Orthodox Judaism, that which marks its difference from traditional Judaism, is the necessity which Orthodox leaders have felt to create institutions and patterns of behavior which would overcome the challenge of secularization inherent in modern modes of thought and behavior. On the other hand, I am not certain that the experience of relativity is as compelling in reality as the Bergers suggest. The seductive quality of the Bergers' formulation may stem from its particular appeal to intellectuals and academicians who do experience "relativity" as an aspect of their reality. It is also possible that the Bergers' definition of modernity doesn't exactly fit the condition of contemporary Orthodoxy because we now live in a post-modern rather than a modern world, a point to which I will return.

My purpose, however, is not to quarrel with the Bergers. On the contrary, I want to emphasize the importance of the term "experience" which recurs three times in their formulation. I emphatically agree that it is the discontinuity between experience (though not necessarily the experience of relativity) and belief, or world view, which poses a major challenge to religion in the modern world. The term "experience" does not refer to particular events, even critical ones, but rather to the daily life one leads and the taken-for-granted conceptual structure which both conforms to and explains that world. It is in this sense that Eliezer Goldman speaks of the "life-world" of pre-modern Judaism as having been

> permeated with elements derived from the dominant religious traditions . . . which was not perceived as possessing causal structure [so that] much that transpired was, as a matter of course, imputed to divine providence. Disease and misfortune could be considered acts of divine retribution in a literal sense. The social and political order was divinely ordained.[5]

The modern world is experienced as a world of cause and effect and of regularity, so there is less room for God's presence, and no need for the God hypothesis to explain what is happening. The contemporary world which we experience is one of less absolute authority, less and less rigid divisions and distinctions, more and more shades, nuances and flows. In short, we experience a world which is discontinuous with traditional Jewish conceptions of an immanent, caring, intervening God or a *halakhic* world view built upon conceptions of authority, absolute right and wrong, and distinctive categories of morality and immorality, purity and pollution.

By posing the problem as one of discontinuity between experience and belief we are saying that modernity, whether viewed as a system of social change and/or a mode of apprehending oneself and reality, does not necessarily undermine religious beliefs and rituals. But it does challenge traditional religion and forces religion to formulate new conceptions and new structures to deal with the challenge.

Let us take *Birkat haMazon*, the Grace After Meals, as an example. Focusing on one discreet ritual is of course misleading, because the argument that modernity challenges traditional religion deals with the entire context of experience as a challenge to the religious world view taken as a whole. Nevertheless, I think this example is instructive.

The Jew is enjoined to recite a series of blessings following a meal. The first blessing praises God who nourishes the entire world with goodness, grace, loving kindness and mercy. The prayer then repeats that God nourishes and sustains all, benefits all and even prepares food for all his creatures.

What possible meaning can such a statement have for a modern person? Tradition ascribes the blessing to Moses, who taught it to the People of Israel as an expression of gratitude to God for the manna which He prepared for them during their sojourn in the desert after they left Egypt and before they entered the Promised Land. The blessing conforms to experience in a primitive agricultural society, in which the farmer is never sure if he will have enough to eat, where his fate is in the hands of indeterminate forces such as weather, tax collectors and brigands. Under such conditions, it is consistent with experience to express gratitude to God for a satisfactory meal. But what meaning can the blessing have for modern, urban, middle-class man whose nourishment comes from packaged containers selected from the stocked shelves of a supermarket open twenty-four hours a day, seven days a week?

Furthermore, the problem is not only the content of the blessing but the time spent in reciting it. The entire Grace, if recited with some degree of care, even silently, takes about a minute and a half. Ninety seconds may not seem like much time, but it can be if non-Orthodox colleagues are about to get up from a luncheon meeting or you are in the middle of a conversation. How do Orthodox Jews handle the discontinuity between experience (the demands of modern life) and traditional beliefs and expectations?

There are no studies of the topic, but I think I can offer a fair guess as to what many of the Orthodox do. They are inattentive to the specific blessing. Instead, *Birkat haMazon* in its entirety is treated as a ritual of order. Like the blessing(s) recited at the beginning of the meal, the Grace at the end functions to set off the meal and invest the act of eating with special significance, introducing an element of sanctity into an otherwise mundane act. The ritual as a whole may be quite meaningful, although its details may be performed and words recited without conscious thought or even understanding. The Grace itself may also be reduced to a ritual detail which remains significant as part of the larger package of rituals whose meaning derives from its being perceived as the imposition of order and the demand for obedience by God.

This does not resolve the technical inconvenience which having to say the Grace imposes. Furthermore, even Orthodox Jews may resist and resent the intrusion of the sanctified into the mundane. This too may be overcome. I am amazed at the ability of some Orthodox Jews to continue their conversations while reciting *Birkat haMazon*. They not only remain attentive to the conversation but, by grunting at appropriate times and with appropriate inflection, even manage to contribute to the conversation while they simultaneously fulfill their formal ritual obligations. There is a parody or satirical Grace attributed to Bnei Akiva youth in the state of Israel a decade ago. Consistent with the changes taking place among Orthodox youth all over the world (see chapter three) one no longer hears it these days. It went:

> *Barukh ata, ata hazan,*
> *haya taim, aval eyn li zman.*

Which in my very free translation is rendered:

> *Blessed art thou, who gave us this dinner;*
> *though I have to run, the meal was a winner.*

Neither solution is satisfactory from an Orthodox perspective. There are not many theoretical solutions to the problems posed by *Birkat haMazon* and to the broader problems which modernity raises. The one which has engaged the greater attention of scholars, those who deal with liberal Christianity in particular, has been the effort to reconceptualize traditional beliefs and modify traditional practice so that their cognitive content now appears consistent with experience. Orthodox Jewish efforts in this direction have been limited. The ArtScroll introduction to the Grace after Meals (the ArtScroll series of publications is the best example we have of Orthodox efforts to produce a series of sacred texts for the English-speaking reader which assumes no prior knowledge of the tradition) simply affirms that:

> there only *seems* to be a difference between the manna on the desert floor and the dainties on the bakery shelf. One is *apparently* a gift from God while the other is the result of the farmer's toil and the processor's guile, but *in reality* both are identical. (emphasis added)[6]

In other words, experience is deceptive. It is possible, of course, that the very recognition of the difficulty is sufficient to combat it. "I know," the ArtScroll commentator seems to be saying, "that this blessing appears anachronistic. But that is because you, the reader, are deceived about the nature of reality." This explanation may be enough for the modern reader. If all truths are relative, if modernity enjoins us to remain open to all possible meanings, if truth is what works for us, then insisting that something is true even though it doesn't appear to be true may suffice, if we want it to be true.

However, the major Orthodox effort has come in other directions. It has sought to restructure experience to conform to traditional belief. Here the closed institution of the yeshiva plays a critical role. Young men and (increasingly) young women spend their formative years (high school and, increasingly, post-high school) in a closed environment, in which not only the ideas they hear but the experiences they undergo conform to traditional beliefs implicit in the *halakhic* conception of the world.

To return to the example of *Birkat haMazon*: The yeshiva is a world in which one "makes" time to say Grace or, more appropriately, Grace is said in its time. But it is also a tenuous world. The yeshiva sustains or nourishes the student spiritually, and sometimes materially, and its survival is sufficiently problematic, its sources of support sufficiently tenuous, that expressing gratitude to God for what the yeshiva provides is not an empty expression. In a larger sense, the yeshiva experience reaffirms in a variety of ways the central structure of the halakhic world view.

Furthermore, that which takes place in the yeshiva is central, that which takes place outside its walls is peripheral. As Menachem Friedman points out, the yeshiva is:

> the true center of existence, in contrast to everything else, which is seen as simply the *s'vivah* [periphery] in which everything is imaginary, and whose sole raison d'etre is to make possible the existence of the center.[7]

As I have suggested, the *halakhic* world view takes as a given the propriety and obviously the existence of authority and obedience, the possibility of living a life of sanctity and purity, a conception of rigid boundaries between good and evil, right and wrong, between insiders and outsiders. It projects the notion of a life without compromise. Not only by what it teaches, but also primarily by its very existence as a closed structure, the yeshiva imparts an experience which conforms to this world view. To a far lesser extent, life within the Orthodox synagogue-community replicates this experience. Actually, the synagogue-community is a major instrument in reinforcing group cohesion and sustaining beliefs or behavior acquired at an earlier period or modeled upon the yeshiva world.

But it is the yeshiva, the closed institution, which is the precondition for Orthodoxy's survival. We must recall that this is the first generation in over 200 years (that is, since its first formulation as the effort by traditional Judaism to confront modernity) in which Orthodoxy is not in decline. Now I may be a social scientist, but at least I am not a reductionist. I reject the notion that political or social or economic factors alone can account for religious change. But it is surely reasonable to ask whether environmental factors may not help account for dramatic changes in the fortunes of Orthodoxy. And I think they do. They include modernity itself. The very absence of rigid ideational and cultural structures which characterizes modernity, the undermining of overarching moral visions and the celebration of plural beliefs and styles of life, invite culturally deviant movements. Secondly, and more specifically, I think the relative success of Orthodox Judaism in sustaining itself numerically in the last two or three decades is attributable in part to the challenge which modern life poses to family stability. I am aware that divorce, not to mention adultery, wife abuse and child molestation, are not unknown in the Orthodox community. But I am impressed, I should say overwhelmed, by the importance Orthodox Jews attribute to family and the extent to which they utilize religious ritual, consciously or unconsciously, to integrate their families. This was not necessarily true in the past. Indeed, the anecdotal literature suggests that the opposite may have been the case.[8] But I believe it is true today. Like Christian fundamentalism, Orthodox Judaism is perceived by its adherents as an importaant basis for family stability.

There are other factors that account for Orthodoxy's success as well. But I want to emphasize what I believe is the most important single factor: the transformation of the yeshiva from an elitist institution designed to prepare *talmidey hakhamim* (masters of Jewish text) to an institution geared to absorb *all* Orthodox Jews. Its latent function is the imposition of a set of experiences which demonstrate the continuity of traditional conceptions about the nature of reality with the life of this world. Those who undergo the yeshiva experience are no longer necessarily rabbis performing a clerical function, but members of local Orthodox synagogues who increasingly set the tone for normative Orthodox behavior even if they are still a minority of synagogue members.

On the other hand, the reliance upon closed institutions means that Orthodox Judaism is necessarily built upon a select group. If my argument is correct, Orthodox Judaism had to withdraw from the larger, more amorphous, non-cohesive Jewish community which became culturally linked to the larger world in the modern period if it was to build institutions to counteract the experience of modernity.

Withdrawal is what I referred to as rejectionism in the previous chapter. As I indicated there, it was not the only option available in responding to the challenge of modernity. Given the circumstances under which Orthodoxy arose, however, it was the only viable one. But it was and still remains a problematic response. It depends on a very strong sense of commitment and the ability to isolate large groups of young people over an extended period of time. In this respect there are limits to the recruitment potential of the yeshiva. No less serious than the impracticality of restructuring experience over the long run for large groups of people is the inherent problem of surrendering a dominant or leadership role in the larger Jewish community, which the withdrawal from and rejection of modernity demands. For the spiritual if not the material welfare of the entire Jewish community is of central importance within the Jewish tradition itself. This explains the excitement about and exaggeration of the number of *baaley tshuva*, those who choose to be Orthodox although they come from non-Orthodox homes and did not undergo Orthodox socialization. But the belief that a resurgent Orthodoxy can sweep Jewish life or even leave an impact upon Judaism the way fundamentalism has left an impact on Christianity or Islam is, I believe, mistaken. Of course, since we social scientists have been so wrong in the past we ought to be very cautious about predicting the future. So let me cautiously suggest that it seems unlikely because Orthodox Judaism, at least in the Diaspora, unlike Islam or Christianity in Muslim and Christian societies, does not emerge from beliefs or behavior patterns current in the society; it doesn't touch base with basic cultural themes. The movement of *tshuva* among Israeli Sephardic or Oriental Jews is the exception. There we have rabbis able to appeal to basic themes prevalent in the folk culture rather than appealing to a counter-culture experience. My central point however, is to observe that the welcome, however halting and suspicious, offered by the yeshiva world to the *baaley tshuva* movement indicates how unsatisfactory are the consequences of a response which leaves Orthodoxy bereft of influence over the larger Jewish community.

The alternative to rejectionism, as I indicated in the last chapter, is affirmationism. One alternative to the "closed institution" is to transform society. This is the first form of affirmationism. In other words, if Orthodoxy must restructure experience in the modern world in order to survive, it can do so either by withdrawing and creating closed institutions or by expanding to control the world and thereby hope to control the nature of people's experience. The transformationist response is only applicable in Israel where one can conceive, farfetched through it may be, of the instrumentalities of control in the hands of the Orthodox. It is associated with the name of Rav Kook (Rabbi Abraham Isaac haCohen Kook, (1865–1935), a preeminent thinker rather than a man of action. In his case, transformation involved reconceptualization. For example, Rav Kook sanctified the activities of the secular Zionist settlers, reinterpreting the nature of modernity by attributing a religious teleology to it. But in the last two decades, in the hands of his late son Rav Zvi Yehuda Kook (1891–1982), and especially in the hands of the son's supposed followers (not all who count themselves among his spiritual legatees are acknowledged as such by others), it has literally meant the transformation of the world. Here is what Rabbi Eliezer Waldman, a former leader of the Yeshiva in Kiryat Arba near Hebron and today a member of the Knesset, said at the time of the war in Lebanon:

> Order in the world will be determined by us. After all, that is what God wants. The inner order of the world, the moral order, the order of faith will be determined by Jews. . . . But can one attain this internal order without concern for external order, opposing evil, military valor? And we shall determine this order as well. We have already begun to do so. . . . We will definitely establish order in the Middle East and also in the world. . . . After all, who will establish order in the world? The leaders of the West with their weak personalities? Do you really think they will determine the order of the world?[9]

Impatience, perhaps frustration with the lack of success of the transformationist effort, coupled with the fervent belief in its practicality, leads its adherents deeper and deeper into the world of politics and power and to the sanctification of instrumentalities (for example the state and the army) which are, in practice, secular.

Despite its shortcomings, the transformationist model is extremely attractive to many Orthodox Jews. Even in the United States an Orthodox rabbi writes that "the task of any generation is to 'Toraize' the culture of that generation."[10] In Israel it has influenced the rejectionist, non-Zionist *haredi* yeshiva world and helps account for their recent aggressiveness.

There is a second, ideal typical form of affirmationism in addition to the transformationist response. I will call this "modernism." Modernism refers to the effort to reconceptualize traditional beliefs so that they appear consistent with modernity; efforts, for example, to demonstrate the equality of women in Jewish law, or the legitimacy of plural interpretations of Judaism, or freedom of choice in *halakha*. Modernism is really a school of thought, as I use the term. It is a manner of conceptualizing Judaism. Some modernists are more radical, others more conservative. They are not necessarily more lenient or permissive in their interpretation of Jewish law, although this is generally the case. But it seems to me that Rabbi Samson Raphael Hirsch and the nineteenth century movement in Germany known as neo-Orthodoxy also falls under this rubric. By modernism I do not mean *halakhic* laxity. I reserve this form of behavior for what I will subsequently call adaptationism.

Modernism's leading figure for many years was Rabbi Emanuel Rackman, now chancellor of Bar-Ilan University in Israel. I would include Rabbi Norman Lamm, president of Yeshiva University and Sir Immanuel Jacobowitz, chief rabbi of the British Commonwealth among its leading exponents, the latter of a more conservative bent. One of the best of the modernist thinkers is Eliezer Berkovits and the roster also includes the fine philosopher Michael Wyschograd. The most radical of all of them is David Hartman. Hartman, through his books and articles, through the Shalom Hartman Institute which he directs in Jerusalem and not least through the very favorable publicity he receives in the *New York Times* has done more than anyone else to spread a conception of Orthodox Judaism which affirms some of the regnant values of contemporary western civilization including the autonomy of the individual, religious pluralism and Jewish nationalism. Hartman is particularly important in my view because his message also carries practical implications. But his impact has been very limited. His ideas strike me as imaginative and sometimes brilliant but he is far better known and more influential among non-Orthodox than he is among the Orthodox. In the eyes of many Orthodox, thinkers such as Hartman appear too apologetic. They stretch the meaning of traditional texts beyond the limits of credulity and they challenge rabbinic authority which is the basis of Orthodoxy's claim to the mantle of tradition. But most devastating of all, they don't interest more than a handful of intellectuals within the Orthodox community. Hartman and others like him are not so much challenged by their Orthodox opponents as ignored. And they are ignored because the rejectionists sense they can afford to ignore them.

The paradox is that the voice of Orthodoxy among the non-Orthodox, particularly in public forums, is generally heard from the mouths of the modernists. Only they will meet with Conservative and Reform rabbis, lecture in Conservative and Reform synagogues or negotiate a mutually acceptable stance with Conservative and Reform leaders. The modernists also tend to be more comfortable in the presence of secular Jews than their more traditional counterparts within Orthodoxy. Class as well as theology plays a role here. Finally, the non-Orthodox prefer the modernist rabbi who can articulate Orthodox conceptions in a terminology which they can understand. The Orthodox rejectionists and their world view often seem so distant that there is little basis for communication.

The popularity of the modernist rabbi among the non-Orthodox may lead him into temptations he finds difficult to resist. He may be so overwhelmed by his acceptance or influence that he finds himself pandering to the non-Orthodox. But the other side of the coin is that the acceptance of the modernist by the non-Orthodox provides him with a certain status in the Orthodox world. Even some rejectionist leaders may turn to a modernist rabbi for help in fundraising for rejectionist institutions. Perhaps it is too early to despair of their influence.

I have stated that restructuring experience is the major Orthodox response to modernity. But this is largely a collective or institutional response. Furthermore, it is an ideal type of response since it falls so far short of being achieved in pure form. In practice, in their own lives, many and probably most Orthodox Jews cope with the challenge of modernity without recourse to either rejectionism, transformationism or modernism in their ideal typical forms.(Furthermore, we must not exaggerate the challenge; for modernity, or at least our "post-modern" world, is in some ways conducive to Orthodox Judaism and other fundamentalisms.) Their strategies, at least in their personal lives, are compartmentalization and/or adaptation. The two strategies are by no means mutually exclusive.

By compartmentalization I mean living in and affirming two distinct worlds. One lives in the sacred, religious, sanctified, halakhic world, the world of the Sabbath, of prayer, of ritual observance and to some extent of family life, by a set of different rules, different conceptions and different images of reality than in the secular world. The Orthodox Jew lives in the secular world as well, and when he does so, in his business or profession, in some of his leisure time activity, in some of his socializing, he may dress, behave and even think no differently than does the non-Orthodox Jew or indeed the non-Jew.The suspension of the intellect that characterizes some aspects of Orthodoxy's response to the Jewish tradition has no relevance for the Orthodox Jew's relationship to other areas of life.

Compartmentalization is sometimes imputed incorrectly to the leader of nineteenth century German neo-Orthodoxy, Samson Raphael Hirsch. Compartmentalization, let it be perfectly clear, has no theological legitimacy in Orthodox Judaism. Orthodox Judaism claims paramountcy for Torah over *all* of one's life. At a practical level compartmentalization also involves problems of dual commitment. The Orthodox compartmentalizers' ideal, I suppose, was an organization of some influence in Orthodox circles in the 1960s, the Association of Orthodox Jewish Scientists. The idealized, largely mythical member of the organization was the scientist (the epitome of modernity) who spent the minimum necessary time engaged in scientific study in order to earn his livelihood or make his brilliant, world-shattering discovery, while he devoted all his remaining time and energy to Torah study. There may have been such people. But I am reliably informed that one can hardly earn a living, much less a reputation as a renowned scientist, with minimal commitment to one's work. The problem with the compartmentalization approach is that by allowing for a neutral, non-sacralized realm in the life of the individual, it opens the possibility that this will become the realm that engages most of one's devotion. In that case Torah study or Judaism, though observed in the most punctilious manner, becomes peripheral. The salvation of the compartmentalization approach, the reason it is in fact so feasible, is that most professional and certainly most business roles no longer demand the kinds of vocational-identity commitments they once did.

Middle class, second generation American Orthodox couples raise their children with the same permissiveness that characterizes their non-Orthodox counterparts, with one important exception. On issues dealing with Jewish matters, particularly Jewish law, they are not permissive. Not only are certain matters forbidden in absolute, non-negotiable, non-compromising terms, but in matters involving Judaism in general and observance of Jewish law in particular, the parents' whole attitude toward the child changes.

What happens, I think, is that parents who like to think of themselves as autonomous, all powerful, as setting the rules by which the child must abide, find themselves in a realm where they have no primary authority but are really only surrogates for the Jewish community, for tradition and in some ways, for God. This unconscious orientation, which can be acted out in different ways is conveyed to the child who learns from the earliest age that things Jewish are quite different from things non-Jewish. I am not suggesting that parent-child relationships don't spill over from one realm to the other. They do. The very permissiveness in the non-Jewish realm is moderated by the fact that there is a realm in which the parents are not permissive. Hence, the child's conception of the world and of society is affected with respect to matters that are ostensibly not Jewish. The relative political conservatism of most Orthodox Jews is related to this. Compartmentalization is never absolute. But it nevertheless exists to some degree and functions as an important component in the identity of the Orthodox Jew.

Compartmentalization refers to separations and distinctions between areas of life but also to different modes of relationships in distinctive areas of life. But it is the process of compartmentalization itself rather than the specific mode of relationship to reality that I think strengthens the survival potential of Orthodox Jews and can serve as a lesson to the non-Orthodox. For compartmentalization instills the sense that the Jewish aspects of one's life are different and set apart from the non-Jewish aspects and that being Jewish doesn't necessarily have implications for everything a Jew does. The concomitant, after all, is that everything one does has implications for one's Jewishness; a proposition that may be theologically sound but hardly tolerable to those who would preserve Judaism in some form.

I do not believe that the process of compartmentalization has been adequately investigated but I am quite certain it is highly complex, involving a host of psychological and sociological factors. Nevertheless, it seems to me we have enough evidence to justify asking non-Orthodox Jewish educators to take a second look at their own educational predispositions and to consider compartmentalization as a major educational strategy.

Perhaps the proposition is better stated in the negative. Jewish life in the United States, as I try to demonstrate in chapter six, shows signs of erosion. A major source of difficulty, in my opinion, is the effort to characterize Judaism as part of, or as essentially no different from, other aspects of life. It is true that integration of the secular into the sacred, the extension of the sacred to all aspects of one's life is a Jewish value. But assuming there is a priority to values, the current priority item on the Jewish agenda is to ensure that some aspect of one's life remains sacred.

Compartmentalization is no ideal solution. But in practice it is the way many if not most Orthodox Jews conduct their lives. A second strategy for coping with the challenge of modernity is adaptation.

Adaptation, as I will describe it, has the least theological legitimacy within the Orthodox world. I am referring to the behavior of many Orthodox Jews, perhaps the majority, who not only compartmentalize their lives but, even within the realm of the sacred, choose those *halakhot* which they will observe with greater or lesser rigor and those they will ignore (i.e., violate). Such Jews are appropriately defined as Orthodox rather than Conservative or even Reform for a number of reasons. They define themselves as Orthodox, they have commitments and affiliations with Orthodox institutions and, as Sam Heilman and Steven Cohen have shown, the pattern of their observance far exceeds the observance pattern of Conservative Jews.[11] But most important of all, these adaptationists make no effort to legitimate their deviations in ideological terms. This is contemporary middle-class, folk Orthodoxy. In the terminology of the *baalei tshuva* (the Orthodox penitents who are the least likely to be adaptationists), the Orthodox "lifer" (one born into the Orthodox world) can permit himself these deviations because his basic religious behavior pattern, his family life and his synagogue life are firmly embedded in an Orthodox network.

The purist, be he Orthodox or non-Orthodox, Jewish or Gentile, is tempted to dismiss this behavior as weak, unauthentic, incoherent and even sinful. It may be. So let me offer a few sociological observations about the sinful, incoherent, weak and unauthentic Orthodox Jews among whom I number some of my best friends. First, they not only respond to modernity, they respond to currents in the Orthodox world as well. Their deviation from observance of Orthodox norms has followed the changing course of normative Orthodox behavior. As Orthodoxy has moved to the right, demanding greater rigor and less subjectivity in its observance pattern, similar changes are observable among the adaptationists. To borrow a statistical metaphor, the standard error of their deviations has remained constant.

Secondly, the adaptationists are often the exemplary model of Judaism to the non-Orthodox. For it is through the adaptationists that non-Orthodox Jews have their greatest contact with Orthodoxy (though the non-Orthodox probably doesn't knew he is confronting an Orthodox "deviant"). It is largely through the adaptationist that Orthodoxy has retained its influence over many non-Orthodox, despite the stances and postures of the leaders of "authentic" Orthodoxy.

Orthodoxy's current influence is due to a number of factors. The most important one, I believe, is the sense of many non-Orthodox Jews that Orthodoxy is the voice of Jewish authenticity. There is an analogy between the attitude of the affirmationists toward the Orthodox rejectionists (discussed in chapter three), and of the non-Orthodox toward the Orthodox. The analogy is not perfect. But the parallel rests in the sense of many Conservative and Reform Jews (including rabbis) and at least some leaders of secular Jewish organizations (Federations of Jewish Philanthropies in particular), that although they are not Orthodox and don't want to be Orthodox, the Orthodox are the better Jews. (A sense that is in fact empirically verifiable as I indicated in chapter one). That means that they are ready to listen attentively to what the Orthodox have to say about Judaism.

The sense that Orthodoxy is the voice of Jewish authenticity may stem from the fact that Orthodoxy is a legitimate expression of the Jewish tradition by everyone's standard whereas Orthodoxy denies that status to Conservatism and Reform (analogous again to the relationships between the Orthodox rejectionists and affirmationists). More important is that Orthodoxy speaks with a sense of confidence about its Jewishness that the non-Orthodox lack.

Indeed, Conservatism and Reform have institutionalized their doubts and ambiguities about the tradition. Reform stresses the individual's freedom to choose which traditional practices are to be observed without passing judgments on that choice. This emphasis finds increasing resonance within the Conservative movement to the point where some statements and behavior of their leaders are indistinguishable from Reform.

But many within the Reform movement and surely many of the crypto-Reform Jews in the Conservative movement must sense that the "freedom of choice" which they glorify is contrary to the basic Jewish tradition which affirms the value of obedience to Jewish law even before one knows the particulars, much less the reasons, behind the law. The "freedom" is more likely a substitute for doubts which many Conservative and Reform Jews harbor about what precisely a Jew is obliged to do and/or the virtual impossibility of imposing what they do think every Jew ought to do. Orthodoxy, on the other hand, makes no overt theological concessions to frailty (the adaptationist acts out his frailty without doctrinal legitimation) nor has it institutionalized any doubts its adherents may share about the implications of the Jewish tradition.

Further, if one is going to pick and choose those aspects of the tradition with which one is most comfortable, which best suit one's needs, psychological make up, and so on, Orthodox Judaism is attractive because it affirms the full gamut of the tradition. Orthodoxy by definition offers the broadest assortment of wares. If Judaism is a cafeteria, why patronize an establishment with a limited assortment? Moreover, from the perspective of the non-Orthodox, Orthodox Jews have made the greatest sacrifices on behalf of their Jewishness. The life style of the Orthodox Jew, his adherence to Jewish dietary regulations or Sabbath law, for example, is an indication of self-sacrifice and commitment that many non-Orthodox find particularly admirable because they lack the willpower to adhere to these same restrictions. The Orthodox have become Jewish role models not because of the specific Jewish laws and prohibitions they observe but because they observe any Jewish law.

The influence of Orthodoxy may also be attributable to the feeling among many non-Orthodox that the Orthodox are the real Jewish survivors. They are the ones least likely to assimilate. As spiritual survival of American Jewry emerges as the latent if not the manifest goal of Jewish organizations in the United States it stands to reason that Orthodox status and hence Orthodox influence has expanded.

But there is also much that the non-Orthodox dislike about the Orthodox. Their manner of dress, their pre-modern conceptions, their rigidity are unattractive and even repellant to many Jews, but most objectionable of all is the absence of tolerance which the non-Orthodox find among them, their rejection of any norms, values, beliefs and modes of behavior which don't bear the Orthodox stamp of approval and most especially their refusal to recognize Conservative and Reform Judaism as authentic or legitimate Jewish expressions. In other words, their extremism. The adaptationists witness to the fact that one can be Orthodox without partaking of these negative qualities.

My third sociological observation is that it is through the adaptationists that Orthodoxy has penetrated the ranks of American Jewish leadership. Philanthropists, communal officers, Jewish organizational professionals and, not least important, Judaic scholars, if they are Orthodox at all, are likely to be adaptationists. Together they have made the American Jewish community a much more Jewishly vibrant community today than it was twenty or thirty years ago.

Finally, my own observations lead me to suspect that the adaptationists constitute a major segment among the rank and file of Jewishly committed Americans and Zionistically committed Israelis. In other words, the adaptationists are among the best citizens of the Jewish polity. It is they who compose a core group of the audience at solidarity rallies on behalf of Soviet Jews or mass demonstrations on behalf of Israel. And they constitute a core constituency for the Jewish day school movement in the United States.

Traditional Judaism has been reshaped by modernity. We call it Orthodox Judaism. There is no reason to believe that this reshaping or reformulation will not continue, particularly as modernity itself assumes new forms. Nevertheless, the continuity between Orthodox Judaism and the tradition is clear both to the outside observer and to the Orthodox Jew. The tradition is expressed in commitment to the authority of Jewish law, however partially that commitment may be made in the case of the compartmentalist, however sparingly in the case of the adaptationist. At the very minimum there is the sense of the absolute authority of the law; this is what defines Orthodox Judaism as a movement and distinguishes the Orthodox individual from the non-Orthodox.

In the modern world, sensitivity, not to mention commitment, to the absolute authority of the law requires the Orthodox Jew to distinguish his (or her) behavior and beliefs, however partially or sparingly, from the behavioral and belief patterns of those around him. One cannot be an Orthodox Jew and be entirely "of this world." Orthodoxy requires a commitment and investment which, in themselves, distinguish the Orthodox Jew from his surroundings. In this respect, the condition of the Orthodox Jew is the opposite of the historical condition of the traditional Jew. For being traditional, whatever else it may be, has always meant living one's life in accordance with rhythms which appear natural and in harmony with reality. This is the paradox of Orthodox Judaism today.

Notes

1. George M. Marsden, *Fundamentalism and American Culture* (New York: Oxford University Press, 1980).
2. Martin Marty in his review of *The Sacred in a Secular Age*, ed. Robert Wuthnow in the *Journal for the Scientific Study of Religion* 25 (September 1986):376.
3. Peter Berger, *The Heretical Imperative* (Garden City, N.Y.: Doubleday, Anchor, 1979).
4. Brigitte and Peter Berger, "Our Conservatism and Theirs," *Commentary* 82 (October 1986):62–67.
5. Eliezer Goldman, "Responses to Modernity in Orthodox Jewish Thought," *Studies in Contemporary Jewry* II ed. Peter Medding (Bloomington: Indiana University Press, 1986), p. 53.
6. *The Family Zemiros*, trans., with marginal notes and introduction by Rabbi Nosson Scherman (New York: ArtScroll Mesorah Publications, 1981), p. 9.
7. Menachem Friedman, "Life Tradition and Book Tradition in the Development of Ultraorthodox Judaism," Harvey Goldberg (ed.), *Judaism Viewed From Within and From Without* (Albany: State University of New York Press, 1987), p. 243.
8. Jacob Katz, in his book *Tradition and Crises* (New York: The Free Press, 1969), notes that the pattern of observance among early hasidim was for adult males to celebrate the holidays in the court of their *rebbe* (spiritual leader) without their families. I have heard older women describe observance patterns in their parents' homes in which women simply waited upon the men during Sabbath or holiday meals without joining them at the table. Religious observance, some of them recall thinking, was an instrument for sexual oppression which they, if not their mothers, resented. I don't know how widespread this feeling was.
9. The statement was printed in a collection of Rabbi Waldman's speeches, *Al Daat Hazman V'hamakom* and cited in the Israeli newspaper *Haaretz* (19 August 1984):14. For further discussion of the article and its significance see my own essay, "Jewish Ultra-Nationalism in Israel: Converging Strands," *Survey of Jewish Affairs 1985* ed. William Frankel (Rutherford: Fairleigh Dickenson Press, 1985), pp. 28–50.
10. Shlomo Danziger, "Jewish Action Symposium," *Jewish Action* 46 (1986):41.
11. Sam Heilman and Steven Cohen, "Ritual Variations Among Modern Orthodox Jews in the United States," Medding, pp. 164–187.

5

Traditionalists and Transformationists

Charles Silberman's recent book, *A Certain People*,[1] has triggered a lively discussion among American Jews about the current state of American Jewish life and its prospects. Silberman's book is a popular, albeit a thoughtful and perceptive presentation which views the state of American Jewish life today with a great deal of satisfaction and describes its future prospects on a high note of optimism. Uziel Schmelz and Sergio Della Pergola[2] borrowing the term from Marshal Sklare, have termed Silberman, along with a group of American Jewish sociologists who view American Judaism from a similar perspective, as "revisionists." The term "revisionist" is an apt one but I want to argue that more is being "revised" than Schmelz and DellaPergola would lead us to believe.

In a landmark essay written almost fifteen years ago,[3] Marshall Sklare observed that almost no non-Jewish sociologist wrote about American Jews. (Since then John Cuddihy has made a notable contribution.) Sklare felt justified, therefore, in using the term American Jewish sociologists in the double sense of sociologists (really social scientists) who are both Jewish and who write about American Jews. That is how I will use the term. Sklare noted that the earliest American Jewish sociologists, writing in the 1920s and 1930s, proceeded from the "belief that the Jewish community was an anachronism prolonged by Gentile prejudice."[4] He called this an "assimilationist perspective." Although this approach did not entirely disappear, a new perspective emerged after World War II which Sklare labelled "critical intellectual." Its adherents were typically radical-leftist in orientation who felt alienated from the Jewish community. Whereas they identified with a romanticized notion of an earlier generation of immigrants, they were contemptuous of contemporary American Jews who had "succumbed to corruptions resulting from a newly achieved class position."[5] Apparently, they were indifferent to the normative question of Jewish survival. Perhaps, they reasoned, since Jews had betrayed their "leftist" or "socialist" heritage, they did not deserve to survive.

61

The third and most recent perspective which Sklare outlined was what he called "survivalist." He cited Glazer, myself and himself as examples of survivalists. The survivalist perspective "looks for evidence of continuity as well as assimilation. Furthermore, it does not uphold assimilation as a desirable objective."[6]

In this respect, all "revisionists" are survivalists. The most obvious of their differences with the "survivalists" (in Sklare's sense) is in their celebration of rather than just sympathy for American Jewish life and their certainty about, rather than simply concern for, Jewish continuity and survival.

The revisionists also differ from the survivalists in their definition of Jewish life. (In this respect they differ from all the American Jewish sociologists who preceded them.) Not all the revisionists are explicit in their redefinition (Silberman least so), but the redefinition is, I think, at least implicit in the level of optimism which they all display.

I want to discuss both types of differences. But before doing so it is helpful to understand the changing climate of opinion in which the studies of American Jewish sociologists take place. Needless to say, climates of opinion may help explain the affinity of certain scholars to certain positions but say nothing about the accuracy of their arguments.

Sociologists, one hopes, are influenced by what they find; but what they find, and the interpretation of what they find is influenced by what they expect to find and what they would like to find. In the case of American Jewish sociologists, this is conditioned by a number of factors, three of which deserve special attention.

First of all, the climate of scholarly opinion concerning the importance of ethnic groups and their capacity for survival has changed dramatically since the late 1960s and early 1970s. The process of modernization was once assumed to include secularization, national-cultural integration and the disappearance of distinctive ethnic or religious subcultures. The present climate of opinion is quite different. The argument is now advanced by a number of scholars (see, for example, Joseph Rothschild[7] or Anthony Smith[8]) that modernization reinforces ethnic identity, distinctive ethnic cultures and ethnic political loyalties. Some students of ethnicity observed as early as the 1960s that American ethnic groups were not disappearing, that American culture buttressed ethnic loyalty.[9] But the argument became far more impressive, virtually compelling, when the scattered observations about particular ethnic groups or the peculiar American experience were now rooted in new theories about the nature of modernization, the kind of global type theory which social scientists find irresistible. If, therefore, regnant theory dictates ethnic resurgence, American Jewish sociologists would expect to find it among American Jews as well.

The fact that some American Jewish sociologists experienced or participated in the Jewish counterculture of the late 1960s and early 1970s may also have prompted them to challenge many older assumptions about the inevitable demise of American Judaism and made them more sensitive to "new forms of Jewish experience." These experiences were probably even influential in directing some young Jews to the choice of Jewish studies as a profession. The growth of Jewish studies in American colleges must have reinforced a sense of Jewish vitality, particularly in the context of earlier predictions about the erosive effect of higher education on Jewish identity. The effect may have been there, but to those who were the exceptions—and in a community as large and diverse as that of American Jews there will always be exceptions—the pessimists must have seemed badly mistaken. Furthermore, as Sklare noted earlier, the pessimism was not only exaggerated but was accompanied by an ideological predilection for assimilation—thereby inviting a counter reaction on the part of Jewishly committed sociologists.

But American Jewish sociologists were and are reacting to a second source of pessimism about the future of American Jews, for not all the pessimists are ideological assimilationists. In the 1970s and 1980s a more pervasive source of pessimism came from Israelis.

It is important to recall that virtually every scholar with any interest in Jewish studies has spent some time in Israel. And contacts with Israelis, certainly discussions on the topic of American Jewry, involves confronting their conviction that this is a community destined to rapid assimilation. This point of view is anchored in a Zionist world view. It is the central article of faith in the Israeli version of Zionism because it provides the most readily available legitimation for *aliyah* (immigration to Israel) and the strongest argument, from a Jewish point of view, against *yeridah* (emigration from Israel). The Israeli case is quite often based on ignorance or a skewed perception of events. Beyond this, however, there is also the suspicion that the "assimilationist" perspective in Israeli hands serves as a weapon to delegitimize Diaspora "interference" in Israeli affairs or American Jewish initiatives in world Jewish affairs which many Israelis believe is their exclusive prerogative. It is not surprising that such attitudes invite a counter reaction whose emotional intensity may cloud disinterested judgment.

Finally, American Jewish sociologists are experiencing a period of unprecedented prosperity. Teaching positions are available in colleges and universities; the Jewish lecture circuit offers very respectable renumeration; demographers, in particular, find their skill in demand by communities anxious to conduct self-surveys or plan for the future; and other social scientists secure additional income as consultants to Jewish organizations. Such a climate of prosperity coupled with the increased status of Jewish social scientists within the Jewish community lends credence to an optimistic perspective. It recalls the different assessment of the future of Jewish life offered by Yiddish language and Hebrew language writers at the turn of the century. The former relative to the latter had better possibilities for publication, enjoyed higher incomes and benefitted from higher status. It is not surprising, therefore, that they assessed the state of the community through rosier colored glasses. It didn't make one group right and the other group wrong but it does help explain the affinity of one group to an optimistic assessment and the affinity of the other group to a pessimistic assessment.

Before I turn to the issues which divide the revisionists from an earlier generation of American Jewish sociologists, the survivalists in particular, I want to relabel the two groups of Jewish social scientists. In a forthcoming study, Steven M. Cohen calls the survivalists "traditionalists" and the revisionists "transformationists." I will adopt his terminology despite the fact that I have used the term transformationist in chapter four to define a subtype of Orthodox Jewish affirmationist. I don't think there is any danger in confusing the terms since the context in which they are used should make their reference very clear. The term "traditionalist" is especially suitable for the survivalists because, as will become evident in the material that follows, traditionalists measure the state of Jewish life against some model, however vague and undefined it may be, of the Jewish tradition. The term "transformationists" suits the revisionists because, as I will argue, they not only assume that Jewish behavior will change but they are inclined to assess these transformations in a positive light and assume that they are evidence of Jewish continuity.

I want to turn my attention now to the issues which divide traditionalists from transformationists; issues which can be treated under three headings.

Quantitative Issues

It might appear strange that professional sociologists should assess quantitative data in different ways. But, first of all, sociologists do not agree about the appropriate measures to assess such ostensibly quantifiable phenomena as intermarriage or Jewish fertility. Second, even if they agreed about exactly what ought to be measured, the data do not exist and they must rely on substitute measures. Finally, even if there were agreement on measures and hard data were available, differences might still arise over their interpretation. What is a lot, what is a little, what is an improvement, what is a decline, what is stability? Economists, for example, who do agree about how to measure the state of the economy, and do have the data available to them, still disagree about what they mean. The *New York Times* (25 May 1986), after observing that the American economy grew at a 3.7 percent annual rate in the first quarter noted that economists interpreted the figure "variously as weak and strong."

It is no surprise, therefore, that American Jewish sociologists interpret their data differently. But they do have data about which they can argue. The severest conflict is over Jewish birthrates, intermarriage rates and the consequences of intermarriage for the Jewish identity of the children. These are significant issues because they have alarmed almost everyone concerned about the future survival of American Jews.

The transformationists deny the validity of the evidence that low fertility or relatively high intermarriage rates threaten American Jewish life. They present contrary evidence which some of them sometimes claim is simply not alarming and at other times claim is actually reassuring. (For example, they sometimes claim that intermarriage both strengthens and increases the size of the Jewish community.)

I do not pretend to any competence in assessing the data. For what it is worth, I found the original transformationist reports (those by Steve Cohen, Goldscheider and Silberman) unconvincing. I harbored reservations about the authors' assumptions, their methodology, and the conclusiveness of their data. It seems to me now, after reading the recent paper by Schmelz and DellaPergola, that the transformationist case has been effectively rebutted.[10] However, in all fairness, it should be pointed out that as of this writing the transformationists have not yet had time to reply to their critics. Furthermore, even if the transformationists are wrong, the data themselves do not point to the disappearance of American Jews. They do point to a very different kind of community and they do justify a sense of concern over the future of the American Jewish community.

Qualitative Issues

A second set of issues can be grouped under the category, "the quality of Jewish life." I discuss some aspects of this question in greater detail in the next chapter. The transformationists themselves admit that one can find evidence for a qualitative decline in Jewish life. This includes a decline in ritual practice and affiliation with conventional Jewish institutions (synagogues, philanthropic campaigns and formal organizations), less social segregation,[11] "ineffective, inadequate and unsuccessful Jewish education, pervasive ignorance . . . about things Jewish and Israel . . . decline in temple and synagogue participation," and "the emphasis on and acceptance of minimum Jewish commitments and the mobilization of energies for fundraising devoid of Jewish content . . . (as) substitutes for creative Jewish commitments."[12]

But the transformationists choose, rather, to stress the positive side of the ledger: the fact that both the Orthodox and the Reform movements have become more traditional, that the Jewish philanthropic world increasingly supports Jewishly particularist activity, that philanthropic and communal leaders are more personally involved in Jewish life, that Jewishly particular symbols (Israel, the Holocaust) have replaced American symbols in Jewish public life and that Judaica courses on college campuses are on the rise.[13] In other publications transformationists point to the *havurah* movements, the growth of political activism among Jews on behalf of Jewish causes, advances in Jewish learning and intellectual life, involvement with Israel and the admission that whereas much of this activity involves a Jewish elite, it is elites which determine the nature of communal life.[14] Moreover, it is argued, by Goldscheider and Zuckerman, for example, that the very visibility of America's Jews is both an expression as well as a source of sociopolitical power and influence which cannot be found in a community in decline.[15] Many of these points and others are elaborated upon and illustrated with anecdotal detail in Charles Silberman's book. His central thesis is that with the decline of antisemitism in the United States, Jews have no reason to conceal their Jewishness and the result is a flourishing Jewish community.

I don't believe that the most critical debate between transformationists (at least among the more moderate of them) and traditionalists (at least among the more moderate of them) takes place over this particular set of issues, except by indirection. Traditionalists might place greater emphasis on certain qualities and less on others. Their overall assessment might be somewhat less sanguine than the transformationists, but both sides would, probably, concede much to the other. However, as we shall see in the next section, definitional and methodological questions which do divide traditionalists from transformationists have implications for assessing the quality of Jewish life.

Methodological and Definitional Issues

The transformationists, I have suggested, also have a special definition of Jewishness. This definition, I believe, rests behind the optimism with which they view the community. It allows them to look for sources of strength and vitality where traditionalists would not have troubled to look and to discount sources of weakness which traditionalists deem significant. None of the transformationists consistently subscribe to this new definition. Among some (Silberman, for example), it generally remains unstated, but it emerges in his penchant for anything new in Jewish life as well as in his reservations about traditional forms of Jewish expression. Among others (Cohen) it just bubbles beneath the surface; in Goldscheider and Zuckerman it is most explicit. My examples, therefore, are drawn from their two books.

Goldscheider and Zuckerman define the vitality or quality of Jewish life by what they call the "cohesion of the community." Jews, the authors claim, interact with other Jews in families, neighborhoods, schools, at work, in organizational and political activities in addition to religious activities.

> The strength of the Jewish community reflects the number and intensity of ingroup interactions. The more the bases of interaction and the greater its intensity, the more cohesive is the community.[16]

What Goldscheider and Zuckerman argue, and in this respect they are not representative of other transformationists, is that Jewish life and survival depends upon structural forces embedded in society which operate independently of the will to survive or the values of the Jews (the "qualitative" factors discussed above.)

> The issue of Jewish continuity in the process of modernization is not primarily related to shared values, communal consensus, or to the desire of the Jews to survive as a community. Nor can it be attributed to the will (or lack thereof) of the broader American community to accept or integrate the Jew. Of primary importance are the patterns of residential clustering, strong occupational and education concentrations, extensive institutional networks and the absence of internal conflicts.[17]

What emerges very clearly, is that Goldscheider and Zuckerman attribute a dominant role to structural factors: "Our analysis points directly to the power of structural factors over values, ideologies and preferences as explanations of the patterns of communal change and levels of cohesion among Jewish communities"[18] or "structural factors condition choices of personal lifestyle."[19]

What concerns me in particular are the implications of this analysis. Whereas the exclusive emphasis on structure as a causal factor is peculiar to Goldscheider and Zuckerman the implications, I believe, are shared by the other transformationists. Only Goldscheider and Zuckerman use "cohesion" as the defining characteristic of Jewishness but other transformationists share their tendency to focus upon what Jews do and assume that activity itself assures the vitality of Jewish life. Traditionalists, on the other hand, are inclined to evaluate some forms of Jewish activity as stages in a process of assimilation, a point which I elaborate upon further in the next chapter.

My argument with the transformationists is that they deny an essential Judaism. In all fairness, Goldscheider does distinguish Jewishness from Judaism,[20] implying that Judaism refers only to the Jewish religion. It is Jewishness, the interaction of Jews with one another, which interests Goldscheider and Zuckerman. Judaism may be dying, but Jewishness is alive and well; it is only being transformed, as the authors continually reassure us. But what this means is that Jewishness can survive without Judaism. The transformationists eschew a discussion of Judaism by which I mean what Jews ought to value and believe and practice or at least what they affirm as the beliefs and values and practices of the Jewish tradition and confine themselves to a discussion of what Jews do. The argument that we can study the one without the other is problematic to say the least. Contrary to Goldscheider and Zuckerman, it seems to me that the term "transformation" which they use so often applies to Judaism, not to Jewishness. It is American Judaism that is being transformed. This, I believe, is what the transformationists are really celebrating, but if they admit this, they must abandon the aura of objectivity.

In defining the areas in which Jewish cohesion occurs, no one area is judged more significant than another. Earlier Jewish sociologists had observed that acculturation and assimilation were processes that took place in stages. Jews, for example, abandoned their distinctive beliefs or culture in the early stages. Their associational ties to one another were the last to be abandoned.[21] Cultural assimilation, wrote Gordon, precedes structural assimilation.[22] Although he believed that the process was inevitable while Sklare did not, both found it necessary to distinguish areas of cohesion (to use transformationist terminology). Attending synagogue and eating in Chinese restaurants are both activities that bring Jews into greater propinquity. But I do not believe they have the same implications for the strength of Jewish life.

If the content of Jewish life rather than its structure has become less distinctively Jewish, some Jews might find less reason to dissociate themselves from Jewish life. Goldscheider and Zuckerman suggest that this is a source of communal strength. For example, let us follow Goldscheider's argument about intermarriage.

> To the extent that there is increasing acceptance of the intermarried within the Jewish community, the simple association of intermarriage rates and community erosion can be challenged. The incorporation of the non-Jewishly born within the Jewish community implies that intermarriage per se does not automatically result in the weakening of Jewish cohesion.[23]

(David Singer noted some years ago that American Jewry is in no danger of disappearing since the community "will be maintained by the simple device of redefining Jewishness in such a way as to include all kinds of people whose *bona fides* would not previously have been acceptable."[24]

Goldscheider goes on to ask whether there are differences between intermarried and non-intermarried couples. He finds some differences exist but that the sets of couples are becoming more alike. This occurs in part because the younger intermarried are becoming more like the non-intermarried (they have more Jewish neighbors), and in part because the non-intermarried are becoming more like the intermarried (the younger non-intermarried have fewer Jewish friends).[25] I don't believe that the proportion of one's closest Jewish friends is a basic measure of Jewish identity or Jewish commitment or the strength of Jewish life although I am aware of the fact that many Jews and many Jewish sociologists view it in these terms. But I see even less justice in equating this measure with one that measures the proportion of one's neighbors who are Jewish. The "friendship" measure strikes me as far more significant. Not only does Goldscheider equate the two measures, but consistent with his redefinition of Jewishness, he finds that the convergence between intermarried and non-intermarried, even though it is attributable in part to diminished Jewishness on the part of the non-intermarried, is a source of strength. (Elsewhere he describes the shift from Orthodoxy to Reform in similar terms.)[26] In other words, what really counts is that Jews behave like other Jews. How they behave is irrelevant.

The logic of the transformationist position, at least when formulated in these terms, leads to the conclusion that Jewish vitality, a strong community, the quality of Jewish life is independent of fidelity to the Jewish past or the Jewish tradition, in short with fidelity to Judaism. Instead, communal leaders should focus on assuring that Jews interact with one another. Indeed, even Jewish institutions are irrelevant because Jewish interaction is not necessarily rooted in formal Jewish organization:

> Even for Jews who do not actively seek to be Jews, their ties, networks and connections to other Jews through family, friends, neighbors, jobs, schools, and leisure activities are important sources of Jewish communal strength.[27]

Goldscheider and Zuckerman have not redefined Judaism, but by stressing the transformation of Jewishness and ignoring Judaism they have committed an equivalent act.

A recent issue of the American Jewish Committee *Newsletter* reviews the debate over intermarriage, labelling the sides "pessimists" and "optimists."[28] I think it would be a mistake to extend this terminology to the differences between the traditionalists and transformationists. The traditionalists are not distinguished by their pessimism. They preceded the transformationists in acknowledging the capacity of American Jews to survive, although they were not certain that they would do so. "It is apparent to us today," Sklare wrote in 1979,

> that the early conception of an orderly cycle from self-segregation to assimilation was an incorrect prediction . . . Jewish identity is far from disappearing. If anything, the Jewish community, as an organized entity, has gained in visibility in recent decades.[29]

Or, as I put it some ten years ago:

> The impact of America on American Judaism, then, is not so simple or so unambiguous as has sometimes been maintained. American Jews have done more than accommodate themselves to their environment. They have not only transformed that environment in some instances, and resisted it in others, but have even remained utterly indifferent to it in areas that touch their deepest concerns and values as Jews. And therein, perhaps, lies some basis for a continued hope for distinctive Jewish survival.[30]

The important difference between traditionalists and transformationists is not whether Judaism can survive in the United States, but whether there is an essential Jewish (Judaic) quality against which American Jewish life can be measured.

My own formulation of the traditionalist position is as follows: American Jews have certainly transformed Judaism in the United States. That is not surprising. One anticipates that Judaism (the sets of values, beliefs, rituals, ceremonies and behavior patterns to which Jews subscribe) will continue to evolve over time, due partially to acculturation and perhaps also to the creation of defense mechanisms to resist the values, beliefs, ritual, ceremonies and behavior patterns of the societies in which Jews live. But there is a point where Judaism or Jewishness might so transform itself that it can no longer be called Judaism. Hence, it is appropriate to argue that one kind of transformation is more authentically Jewish and another kind is less so. We may disagree sharply over which transformation is more and which is less Jewish. I, for example, believe that Orthodox Judaism in the United States (itself the result of the transformation of the religious tradition) is more authentically Jewish than Reform Judaism. I also think that that which is often called "Jewish liberalism" has very little Jewish authenticity. But I must concede that those who disagree with me can raise very valid objections.

I cannot dismiss out of hand the argument that Conservative or Reform Judaism is a more authentic transformation of traditional Judaism than Orthodoxy, or is at least equally authentic. I am also prepared to acknowledge that liberal and even secular Judaism has a case in seeking to anchor its political orientations in a Jewish world view. The argument as to who is right would be based on the interpretation of texts, the choice and authority of different sources, the relative weight one attributes to different values within the tradition, the most effective requisites for Jewish life, and not least, moral judgments which I acknowledge are influenced by extra-Judaic considerations.

The first question, therefore, is how Jews transform their Jewish tradition. The second question in evaluating American Jewish life is how American Jews align themselves with this tradition. This is the question of Jewish identity and commitment.

If we know the answers to these questions we can arrive at some estimate of the state of American Judaism, though not all estimates will be the same. But we can meaningfully discuss the quality of Jewish life, even if we are indifferent to its survival. That is also why it was entirely appropriate for so eminent a sociologist as Nathan Glazer to conclude his own study of American Jews with a question rather than a definitive statement:

> What is left is a relation to a tradition in which, from all one can tell, the echo once sounded, and there was a readiness to listen. What can still come of it, I do not know.[31]

Glazer may have been too skeptical. He may have been too rigid in his interpretation of the tradition. Thirty years later he assessed the future differently.[32] But he did raise *the* question one must ask if one is concerned about the survival of American Judaism or American Jewish life. It is a question that some transformationists, when they are not behaving as self-conscious transformationists also ask themselves. But the logic of the transformationist argument, even when unintended, is quite different. It denies the relevancy if not the existence of a Judaism of essence. It affirms that ethnicity "emerges in the modern world; it is not the cultural legacy of the past or a fixed primordial quality."[33] Therefore, one need not raise questions about the relationship of American Judaism to the Jewish tradition.

The first task of the sociologist is to describe American Jewish life. This includes the values, beliefs and behavior patterns of American Jews. These will differ from the Jewishness (or Judaism) of Russian, or French or Israeli Jews or the Jewishness (Judaism) of nineteenth-century East European Jews. There may be a point in distinguishing the term Jewishness from

Judaism, though this raises the question of defining Judaism or the Judaic tradition. But once one not only describes American Jewishness but also makes judgments about its quality, its vitality and its future, one must confront its relationship to Judaism. My fear is that the transformationist view unwittingly serves those who would transform American Judaism by severing it from both the Jewish tradition and the rest of world Jewry.

Notes

1. Charles Silberman, *A Certain People* (New York: Summit Books, 1985).
2. Uziel Schmelz and Sergio DellaPergola, "Some Basic Trends in the Demography of US Jews: A Reexamination." Paper prepared for a conference on New Perspectives in American Jewish Sociology, American Jewish Committee, New York, 1986.
3. Marshall Sklare, "The Jew in American Sociological Thought," *Ethnicity* 1 (1974):151–173.
4. Ibid., p. 161.
5. Ibid., p. 165.
6. Ibid., p. 166.
7. Joseph Rothschild, *Ethnopolitics: A Conceptual Framework* (New York: Columbia University Press, 1981).
8. Anthony Smith, *The Ethnic Revival* (Cambridge: Cambridge University Press, 1981).
9. Nathan Glazer and Daniel Moynihan, *Beyond the Melting Pot* (Cambridge, MA: The M.I.T. Press, 1963).
10. Schmeltz and DellaPergola. They also have an article scheduled to appear in volume five of *Studies in Contemporary Jewry.*
11. Steven M. Cohen, *American Modernity and Jewish Identity* (New York: Tavistock, 1983), p. 177.
12. Calvin Goldscheider and Alan Zuckerman, *The Transformation of the Jews* (Chicago: University of Chicago Press, 1984), pp. 186–187.
13. Steven M. Cohen and Leonard Fein, "From Integration to Survival: American Jewish Anxieties in Transition," *Annals of the American Association of Social and Political Science* 480 (1985):81–82.
14. Cohen, pp. 177–178.
15. Goldscheider and Zuckerman, p. 185.
16. Goldscheider, p. 1.
17. Goldscheider and Zuckerman, p. 187.
18. Ibid., p. 240.
19. Ibid., p. 235.
20. Goldscheider, p. 165.
21. Marshall Sklare and Joseph Greenblum, *Jewish Identity on the Suburban Frontier* (Chicago: University of Chicago Press, 1967).
22. Milton Gordon, *Assimilation in American Life* (New York: Oxford University Press, 1964).
23. Goldscheider, p. 14.
24. David Singer, "Living With Intermarriage," *Commentary* 68 (July 1979):53.
25. Goldscheider, p. 26.

26. Ibid., p. 182.
27. Goldscheider and Zuckerman, p. 225.
28. American Jewish Committee, *Newsletter*, Spring 1986.
29. Marshall Sklare, "Jewish Acculturation and American Jewish Identity," in *Jewish Life in America: Historical Perspectives* ed. Gladys Rosen (New York: Institute of Human Relations Press and Ktav, 1979), 169–170.
30. Charles Liebman, "Jewish Accommodation to America: A Reappraisal," *Commentary* 64 (August 1977):60.
31. Nathan Glazer, *American Judaism* (Chicago: University of Chicago Press, 1957), p. 149.
32. Nathan Glazer, *New Perspectives in American Jewish Sociology* (New York: American Jewish Committee, 1987).
33. Goldscheider and Zuckerman, p. 9.

6

The Quality of Jewish Life

The reader who has followed me this far is aware of the personal and subjective nature of much that I have to say. This will be especially true in this chapter where offer my assessment of the quality of American Jewish life. First of all, "quality" is a subjective term. There are no standards for assessing the quality of a peoples religio-ethnic life. Secondly, even if we could agree on such standards we have no criteria by which to measure them. For example, I believe that both a cause and reflection of the decline in the quality of American Jewish life is the decline in the quality of the Conservative and Reform rabbinate. But it may be argued that the quality of the Conservative and Reform rabbinate is not a fair standard by which to assess the quality of American Jewish life. Perhaps the rabbis have been replaced by other types of spiritual leaders so the decline in the quality of American rabbis is irrelevant to the quality of Jewish life or is balanced by other developments in Jewish life. Second, even if one were to agree that the quality of American rabbis is a fair standard by which to judge the quality of Jewish life, how could one demonstrate the decline in the quality of the American rabbi?

Thirdly, the term "quality" is not the only troublesome term. What is meant by "American Jewish life?" Is the reference to the manner in which American Jews conduct their Jewish life? Clearly, there are enormous differences among American Jews ranging from those who have no Jewish life, i.e. nothing they do bears a relationship in their mind or in the mind of others with anything Jewish, to the hasidim of Williamsberg whose entire lives are governed by Jewish imperatives. But perhaps the term "Jewish life" refers to the conduct and policies of the organized Jewish community: to the conduct of various Federations and their constituent agencies, the Jewish defense organizations and their chapters, the Zionist and fraternal Jewish organizations, and so on. Here too the variation is enormous. This chapter which touches on both the private and communal aspects of Jewish life pushes generalizations to the straining point.

Fourth, my assessment is based largely on impressions derived through my own observation or the selection of materials I have read. Observation and selection is necessarily biased toward the idiosyncratic. Our minds register the unusual and not the routine. So the analysis that follows, even if accurate in detail may distort the total picture.

In conclusion, this essay's claim to validity is based in good measure on my own past experience in studying American Jewish life. It was originally commissioned by the American Jewish Committee and written in January 1987. I have spent a good many years in Israel arguing against the view, prevalent there, that American Jewry is destined to assimilate. I still believe that there is nothing inevitable about Jewish assimilation in the United States. In one article I pointed to the complexity of the very terms "acculturation" and "assimilation" when applied to an analysis of the future of American Jewry.[1] In a second, I documented the growing strength of Jewish commitment among Jewish leaders.[2] My current rather somber assessment of the quality of Jewish life in America is not even balanced by the satisfaction I might have had in saying "I told you so." On the other hand, the chapter can only be understood in a particular context. A few years ago I would not have written such an essay. It must be viewed as a response to some recently published and widely acclaimed books which have argued that American Jewish life is flourishing. I am convinced that such assessments are wrong. The fact is that there are positive developments in American Jewish life. But the recent tendency of American Jews, leaders of communal Jewish organizations in particular, has been to pat themselves on the back and glorify their achievements. I find a growing tendency to ignore and even to deny the pathologies of American Jewish life. These pathologies raise serious questions about its quality and signal threats to its future.

Signs of Erosion

I begin by commenting on four aspects of American Jewish life which point to its erosion. I do not believe that all signs of Jewish life point in that direction. But those I have chosen are all central rather than peripheral aspects of Jewish life. There is nothing original in the presentation. But as I suggested, the recent celebratory mood of the American Jewish community is an invitation to recall some bitter truths.

The first aspect worth recalling is the incidence of mixed marriage. Mixed marriage is not the same as conversionary marriage. Mixed marriage refers to marriages between Jews and persons who do not consider themselves Jewish and who have not undergone conversion whether in accordance or not in accordance with *halakha* (Jewish law).

My first observation with respect to mixed marriage is that some American Jews including communal leaders and sociologists ask the question: what is the impact of such marriages on Jewish society? This is not an inherently unreasonable question. It is certainly no less unreasonable than asking: what is the impact of wife abuse on society?[3] But I cannot help note that a more commonsensical and I think healthier question is to begin by observing that there is something intrinsically wrong with wife abuse; it is an evil that ought to be combatted regardless of whether it does or does not adversely affect society. Now some social scientist is going to argue that battered wives are women who really want to be battered, that if no permanent damage is done to the wife there is no justification for the community interfering in private family matters, that it is inappropriate for society in general and social scientists in particular to make value judgments and finally that there is no way society can prevent wife abuse anyway so it might as well learn to live with it. I would respond that such an attitude reflects more than the professional conclusions of a learned scholar. It also tells us a great deal about his values.

As far as the incidence of mixed marriage is concerned, all observers of Jewish life acknowledge that it has risen to very high levels. In a forthcoming study by Bruce Phillips on the Jews of the west coast[4] he finds, as do others in studies of other regions of the United States, that the proportion of mixed marriage to conversionary marriage is continually rising. In Denver and Phoenix, 61 percent of Jews under 30 are married to non-Jewish partners. In Los Angeles the figure is around 30 percent. Steven M. Cohen estimates the nationwide figure at about one-third. Phillips predicts that "the next generation of Jewish children [on the west coast] will include at least as many children from mixed marriage homes as from in-married homes." In comparing the Jewish behavior of mixed marrieds to inmarried couples he finds exactly what we would expect—dramatic differences in their Jewish affiliation and identity.

The second aspect of American Jewish life that points to deep problems is Jewish education. I am impressed by and welcome the growth of Jewish communal support (i.e. Federation support) for Jewish education. But I have also observed that within Federations the discussion of the importance of Jewish education revolves around its contribution to Jewish identity and survival. I would have thought that Jewish education, i.e. knowledge about one's past and one's traditions, knowledge of one's own culture would have been a self legitimating value.

The second and related point is that most of what passes for Jewish education, at least at the supplementary school level is not about the Jewish past, the Jewish tradition or Jewish culture; so perhaps Federation leaders were asking a proper question after all; except that I'm not certain they are familiar with what is being taught in Jewish schools.

Jewish education involves preparation for *bar* or *bat mitzvah* and it is also about learning to be a proud Jew (as though this was something that one can learn in a school) and involving the student in a Jewish experience. The substance and content of the Jewish educational experience which the majority of American Jews undergo is trivial, at best.

An estimated 41 percent of Jewish children between the ages of three and seventeen are enrolled in some kind of Jewish school.[5] Seventy-two percent of them are in supplementary schools where they attend class from two to eight hours a week. Whereas schools under Reform auspices have been increasing the number of school hours per week from two to four, the trend in Conservative sponsored schools is to decrease the number of weekly school hours from eight to six and in many schools to four. In many instances supplementary school principals are the only personnel in the school system with formal training in Jewish education. In some instances even the principal may have little or no formal training. Supplementary school principals in one of the largest Jewish communities in the United States just completed a fourteen week course on educational supervision. The course instructor informed me that "the principals are afraid to walk into the classroom out of fear of what they will confront."

The proportion of all Jewish youth receiving any Jewish education drops from 69 percent of those in grades five to seven (the *bar* and *bat mitzvah* age) to 35 percent of those in grades eight to ten. It falls to 12 percent of those in grades eleven to twelve. In the day school system where Jewish children receive the most intensive form of Jewish education available, only 8 percent of those eligible are in grades eight to ten and 6 percent in grades eleven to twelve.

It has been suggested that Judaica courses at the college level can fill the gap left by inadequate Jewish schooling at the elementary and high school level. There is no evidence to support such a claim.[6] We have no data on the number of Jewish college students enrolled in courses in Judaica much less assessments as to whether college courses are better or poorer alternatives to traditional forms of Jewish education. Furthermore, it seems probable, though we lack data on this point as well, that those who do avail themselves of college courses are those who come with a better and more intense Jewish educational background. I have asked chairmen of Judaica programs to estimate the proportion of Jewish students at their colleges and universities who enroll in at least one course in Jewish studies during their college attendance. Such a figure would at least measure the interest of college students in learning about their own past. My informants stressed that all such estimates were difficult to arrive at. When asked to make a liberal judgement they offered percentages ranging from generally around five percent or less to, in one case, as high as twenty percent. In no case were my informants overwhelmed by the interest of Jewish college students in Judaica courses.

The third aspect of American Jewish life which merits attention relates to Jewish denominationalism and synagogue life. I attribute enormous importance to synagogues. They are the core institutions for the majority of American Jews who are affiliated in one way or another with the Jewish community. Less than half of all American Jews are affiliated with a synagogue; I suspect the figure hovers around 40 percent. But, as I note again below, Jews unaffiliated with a synagogue are unlikely to be affiliated with any other Jewish organization and are less likely to identify as Jews on any credible measure of Jewish identity.

Conservative Judaism has been the numerically largest of the Jewish denominations. The affiliation levels of younger Jews and of third and fourth generation American Jews indicate that Reform may have replaced Conservatism as the largest denomination in Jewish life. But the Conservative movement remains of central importance not only because of its size but by virtue of its centrist position between Orthodoxy and Reform. This has helped prevent Reform from veering too far to the left. Conservative Judaism has served as a moderating or deradicalizing influence on Reform. Hence, one has to be concerned about the sorry state of the Conservative movement.

The growth of Reform at the expense of Conservative Judaism is the first point that deserves comment. We have many surveys which compare American Jews with one another in accordance with a variety of measures of Jewish commitment. Best known are the national surveys conducted by Steven M.Cohen for the American Jewish Committee but there are a number of local studies as well. To the best of my knowledge every study provides the same results. Orthodox Jews score higher than Conservative Jews and Conservative Jews higher than Reform Jews who in turn score higher than unaffiliated Jews on any credible measure of Jewish identity. Synagogue affiliation by denomination or denominational identification (the two are not quite the same since some Jews identify with one denomination and belong to the synagogue of another or identify with a denomination without affiliating with any synagogue) are the best indices we have as shorthand measures of Jewish commitment.[7] So, the growth of Reform Judaism at the expense of Conservative Judaism suggests a decline in commitment among American Jews although, theoretically it may also portend a rise in the Jewish commitment of Reform. My own suspicion is that the relative growth of Reform has a great deal to do with its more permissive attitude toward mixed marriage and its accommodating attitude toward non-Jews within its synagogues.

Secondly, lay leaders in Conservative synagogues report increasing difficulty in recruiting leaders. The president of one synagogue told me that his term of office is only three months since no one in the congregation is willing to take the job for a longer period of time. Terms of office of one year are not uncommon and two years are the norm. My informants stress that this is not a result of the democratization of synagogue life but of the absence of commitment on the part of the membership.

Finally, informants active in Conservative synagogues in different parts of the United States complain about their difficulty in finding suitable rabbis to fill their pulpits. It is their impression that the Jewish knowledge, human skills, general competence and even Jewish commitment (not to mention morale) of the younger generation of Conservative rabbis is below that of a previous generation of rabbis. I want to emphasize that I discussed this matter with only a handful of people. They may be unrepresentative. Perhaps their own standards have risen and that is why they judge the rabbinate so harshly. Of all the observations I make in this chapter this, in my opinion, is the most problematic. But it merits inclusion as reflecting the perception of Conservative leaders with whom I spoke.

The fourth and final aspect of American Jewish life which I raise has to do with Jewish culture. There are positive developments in Jewish cultural life to which I will return in a later section. The point I make here is that the organized Jewish community celebrates as Jewish culture anything written by or about Jews or of interest to Jews without regard to its Judaic content. In other words, Jewish culture is perceived as worthy of recognition and celebration even when that culture bears no link to Judaism or the Jewish tradition however broadly those terms may be defined. I am not, in other words, protesting the level of Jewish culture. In my opinion, "high Jewish culture" is prospering in the United States relative to any other period in American Jewish history and I welcome this development. My reference here is to the organized Jewish community's conception of Jewish culture.

November is "Jewish Book Fair" month and Jewish Community Centers all over the United States in cooperation with other local agencies sponsor events connected to Jewish books. The local community will sponsor visits and lectures by authors whose work the host community wishes to celebrate. In Houston, Texas this has meant that whereas a speaker in one year was Elie Wiesel, in another year it was Erica Jong.[8] I happened to be in Miami in November and was able to read about its 1986 Book Fair. It featured William Novak who lectured twice; once on his book *Iacocca* and once on the "issues addressed in [his book] *The Great American Male Shortage and Other Roadblocks to Romance.* The following day the featured speakers were Francine Klagburn, author of *Married People: Staying*

Together in the Age of Divorce and Peter Hall, a tour operator who "was one of the victims of the TWA hijacking in June 1985 by Shiite terrorists."[9]

Jewish Book month in New Haven (selected because I resided there in 1986–1987), was celebrated, according to the *Connecticut Jewish Ledger*[10] by a "two day festival." The "cultural event of the winter season" was sponsored by the Jewish Community Center, The Department of Jewish Education of the New Haven Jewish Federation, the Jewish Book Shop and the sisterhood of the largest congregation in the area. The festival began on Sunday. According to the local Jewish weekly, the "main attraction [included] humorist Moshe Waldoks, co-editor of the *Big Book of Jewish Humor*, whose topic will be 'Messiahs, Medicine Men and Moveable Furniture.'" I found the *Big Book of Jewish Humor* very entertaining. I am grateful to its editors. Their book is distinctively Jewish. My concern, however, is with an organized community which highlights that book or others with less Jewish content, as centerpieces of Jewish culture.

A Second Look at the Concept of Assimilation

Many American Jewish sociologists today dismiss the possibility of American Jewish assimilation. I think the problem deserves renewed attention. Granted, those who invoked the term in the past were far too glib in predicting the rapid assimilation of American Jews or in the irreversibility of the process. They were mislead by mistaken sociological theory about secularization and modernization just as Israelis are mislead by Zionist ideology in predicting the inevitability of assimilation. Furthermore, the term was and is bandied about without sufficient rigor. The implicit model of assimilation was someone born and raised as a Jew who, at a certain point in his life ceased to think of himself as a Jew. This is not a major problem of the American Jewish community today. Those raised as Jews continue to think of themselves as Jews regardless of how they behave. The acceptance of Jews in American society, the absence of prejudice and discrimination against them and the high status that Jews currently enjoy probably means that fewer Jews today than in the past consciously deny their Jewish identity or consciously seek to escape the stigma of being born a Jew. But this does not mean that assimilation at the individual level is not taking place. It is. First of all, and less important for my purpose, it takes place as a result of mixed marriage. Some of the offspring are not raised to identify themselves as Jews. Others are raised to think of themselves as part Jewish; a form of identity that is more readily discarded. Most problematic are those who are raised to think of themselves as Jewish but also as Christians or raised to believe that it is perfectly appropriate to feel equally at home in a church and a synagogue. We do not know how widespread a phenomenon this is or how it will work itself out in one or two generations but we know that it is taking place.

I am concerned, however, with a more complex model of assimilation; one that may effect substantial numbers of mixed marriage households but also effects substantial numbers of inmarried Jews as well. This is a form of collective assimilation which takes place in stages.[11] The endpoint in such a process may not be the disappearance of American Jews as an identifiable entity. Instead, the reference is to a process of attenuation of ties between American Jews and the Jewish tradition and/or between American Jews as a collective body and the collective body of Jews outside the United States. In this model, which I believe merits more careful attention, Jews do not exchange their identity for some other religion or ethnic group. The key process is not the Jew becoming non-Jew but rather the Jew evolving an identity and a sense of self which blurs his distinctiveness from other Americans while emphasizing his distinctiveness from traditional Judaism or from non-American Jews. The reference here is to the emergence of a Jewish American identity which, like Italian-Americanism or Irish-Americanism is integrated into an American ethnic mosaic but is sharply differentiated in belief and behavior from the Jewish past or the Jewish world.-This form of assimilation is more appropriately labeled transformation, but it is a particular form of transformation since not all forms of transformation have the assimilatory consequences suggested here. The process does not take place in one generation nor is it irreversible. In addition, it need not involve every American Jew. In the present case, it clearly does not, a point to which I will return. Finally, it is a process which is difficult to document because it involves assumptions about core characteristics or essential characteristics of the Jewish tradition or of the Jewish people from which American Jews deviate. Measuring this deviation is also fraught with problems; particularly when the deviationists themselves claim that their behavior is consistent with tradition or necessary in order to preserve other, more essential aspects of the tradition.

For example, I believe that the decision of American Reform Judaism to recognize children of Jewish fathers and non-Jewish mothers as Jewish is a major deviation from the essence of the Jewish tradition and accepted Jewish norms throughout the world. But Alexander Schindler, leader of American Reform Judaism argues that it is both consistent with the tradition as he understands it and necessary in order to preserve Judaism.[12] One's evaluation therefore, depends on one's own conception of Judaism, on the credibility of Schindler's statement[13] and of course, on the outcome of the Reform decision. Nevertheless, I believe that such assessments must be made unless one is prepared to deny that there is any essence to Judaism or that Jewish life has meaning without regard to Judaism. Some social scientists have asserted this proposition.[14] To the extent that Jewish policy makers accept this proposition they seem to me to be furthering the erosion of Jewish life.

To rephrase my position in historical perspective; had late nineteenth-century American Reform Judaism (the Judaism embodied in the Pittsburgh Platform of 1885) triumphed, its legacy would have been an American Judaism devoid of significant distinguishing characteristics, well integrated into upper-middle class American cultural life, retaining only nominal or symbolic Jewish forms. Nineteenth-century American Reform was overwhelmed by the migration of Eastern European Jews to the United States who traditionalized the form and content of Reform Judaism and reintegrated it into the Jewish world and the Judaic past. Therefore, the reemergence or continued vitality of nineteenth-century Reform not only among Reform Jews but among Conservative Jews as well must give one pause.

The following are some illustrations. In an article "Thoughts on *Golus*," written by an American Conservative rabbi, the author says:

> While *Golus* is a Jewish word it is not only a Jewish issue. It is a human issue as well. *Golus* in 1986 is children going to sleep hungry night after night. It is approximately 30 armed conflicts raging around the globe. It is the continuing deterioration of our habitat and ecosystem . . . And most alarmingly, it is thousands of nuclear warheads ready at this moment to annihilate us all.[15]

All the Conservative and Reform synagogues in the New Haven area cooperate in sponsoring a *Tisha B'Av* service. According to the chairman of the evening, "originally the observance of Tisha B'Av recalled only the destruction of the Holy Temple." However, he went on to say, it now includes commemoration of other calamities. Finally, he concluded that:

> This year, in honor of the 100th anniversary of Miss Liberty, special recognition will be included of our great debt to the United States of America for the opportunity that this country has given our people.[16]

At the Pacific Southwest Convention of the United Synagogue of America held in November 1986 a *Supplementary Prayer Book* in English was prepared for the Friday evening and Sabbath services. There were five selections, each of which was recited aloud at various points in the service. Each merits separate discussion but I refer to only two of them here. One, recited after the "Amidah" prayer, was a statement by Jihan Sadat on peace. The final selection was adopted from the new Conservative prayerbook,

Sim Shalom. It is a translation of "Why I am a Jew" by Edmund Fleg and the theme of his creed becomes clear in the following concluding lines:

> I am a Jew because the promise of Judaism is a universal promise. I am a Jew because, for the Jew, the world is not finished: men will complete it. I am a Jew because, for the Jew man is not fully created: men are creating him. I am a Jew because Judaism places man above nations and above Judaism itself. I am a Jew because, above man, Judaism places the oneness of God.

Lest my point here be misunderstood, I don't believe Judaism can survive, much less flourish, unless it evolves. I would be happy to see Judaism evolve into a more open, universalistic, liberal direction. So, in some respects, I welcome many currents in American Jewish life. I believe that, under the proper circumstances, they are especially helpful as an antidote to developments I fear are taking place in Israeli Judaism. But I also believe that one can distinguish between a coherent Judaism which is anchored in a Jewish past even as it redefines that past and with it, the imperatives of the present, and what I sense is an increasingly incoherent pattern of symbols and a random structure of responses that constitute much of American Jewish life. There is no imminent danger that American Jews will abandon their concern with Israel or with Soviet Jewry. On the contrary, much of organized Jewish life today is built around support for Israel and world Jewry. But there is a danger that a conception of American Judaism will develop that will make such support increasingly meaningless and eventually lead to its diminution. Such a process may, in fact, already be taking place.

The Foundations of the Optimistic Perspective

If my observations are correct, how does one account for the very different assessment by other students of American Jewish life? The obvious answer is that our measures of Jewish life and our definition of what constitutes a healthy or flourishing or vigorous Jewish community are so subjective that there is room for a variety of interpretations. The personal biographies of the scholars themselves, their own experiences, their particular ideologies, the environment in which they carry out their studies and even the literature to which they respond all influence their subjective appraisals. This applies to the present paper as well.

What follows are four additional fators I believe have led other observers to assess Jewish life differently than this present assessment. I am not concerned here with questions of ideology or environment some of which I touched upon in the previous chapter.

First, American Jewish life is far more public and communal than it was a few decades ago. Anti-semitism in American public life has declined. American Jews feel more secure today than they did in the past. Furthermore, ethnicity and the display of ethnic symbols is not only legitimate but is valued in American culture. Charles Silberman's *A Certain People*[17] in reminding us how far Jews have come in American society also reminds us of how burdensome Judaism was just one generation ago for those who sought prestige, status and acceptance among Gentiles. Furthermore, the anti-semitism from which the aspiring Jew suffered did distinguish between the Jew who subdued his Jewishness and the Jew who consciously or unconsciously displayed it. Dan Oren's study of the history of Jews at Yale documents this point nicely.[18] One result was a sacrifice of one's Judaism as the price of acceptance but another result was the concealment of one's Jewish identity, its privatization, its removal from the public realm.

Acceptance of Jews and ethnic legitimacy have reduced the pressures to sacrifice one's Jewish identity and rendered its privatization unnecessary. In addition, privatization itself has lost a great deal of meaning in a culture which increasingly blurs lines between public and private life. It is a middle-aged academic from an English university contrasting his generation and culture with young American college students in the late 1960s who observes that:

> We're private people, aren't we, our generation? We make a clear distinction between private and public life; and the important things, the things that make us happy or unhappy are private.[19]

Increasingly, and this remains a legacy of the rebellious countercultural student movement of that period, our dress, our speech, our behavior that was once private has now become public. This is particularly true of Jewish life for an additional reason. Increasing numbers of Jews do not know how to act out their Jewishness in the private domain and depend upon the public domain to express their Jewish identity. This is reflected in two interrelated developments. First, the kinds of ritual and symbolic behavior which were once carried out privately but not publicly are now carried out publicly but not privately. Wearing a yarmulke, reciting a blessing before or Grace after meals is a commonplace at public Jewish functions of all kinds even when none of the participants might do so in the privacy of their homes. References to the Jewish New Year, or Ḥanukkah, or Passover are increasingly heard in the mass media and evoke associations for Jews to whom the Jewish New Year is not a new year in any meaningful sense, for whom Ḥanukkah is at most a surrogate Christmas and Passover the occasion for the extended family to eat together. Secondly, Jews who are increasingly uncomfortable or ignorant of their religio-cultural tradition, a tradition whose primary locus is the home, now favor public, communal and political activities with which they feel more comfortable and/or in which they can engage as spectators.

This public activity, intensified since 1967, can easily deceive us. It renders Jewish life far more visible than in the past and projects a false image of Jewish vitality. Obviously, I welcome such activity. Hopefully it is an instrument to strengthen Jewish life but I am inclined to evaluate it as a form of residual Jewishness rather than an alternative expression of Jewishness as I seek to demonstrate below.

This brings us to the second factor which has led some observers to a benign assessment of American Jewish life. It has been argued that there are alternative modes by which Jews may express their Jewishness. Whereas, it is argued, American Jews may have abandoned one form of expression (e.g. religious belief and ritual behavior), they have substituted others:

> These new forms provide a wide range of options for expressing Jewishness [and include] the combination of family, friends, community activities, organizations, and reading about and visiting Israel.[20]

I have conceptual reservations about this argument. As I already suggested, I do not believe Jewish life can be assessed independently of its relationship to Judaism. But there are strong empirical grounds for rejecting the argument that there are alternative expressions of Judaism in the United States and that one is strengthened as the other diminishes in strength.

The strongest case that can be made for such a proposition is American Jewish support for Israel There is no question that the American Jewish community in general and American Jews in particular have become more interested in and supportive of Israel since 1967. Is this not evidence of a resurgent Judaism? Can it not be argued that Jews are substituting one form of Jewish expression for another? Steven M. Cohen puts the matter as follows:

> In light of the secular roots of Zionism and its broad appeal to the modernizing masses, one might speculate that support for Israel today would be strongest among the ritually non-observant American Jews, who in effect may supplant God with country.[21]

Cohen measures support for Israel through use of three indices: concern for Israel, support for her policies and travel to Israel. He found that younger people were less pro-Israel than their elders and the more ritually observant were more pro-Israel. His forthcoming 1986 National Survey of American Jews reinforces this observation. Paul Ritterband, in his forthcoming study of New York City Jews, arrives at similar conclusions with respect to other forms of Jewish expression including the proportion of one's friends who are Jewish or the number of Jewish organizations to which one belongs. The more ritually observant and synagogue attending the Jew is, the more likely he is to score higher on any credible measure of Jewish identity. There surely are a variety of forms of Jewish expression but the Jew who scores high on one measure is likely to score high on all of them and the Jew who scores low on one measure is likely to score low on all of them. This wasn't true in the past and it need not necessarily be true in the future, but it is true today.

With respect to American Jewish support for Israel I would argue that it is the lowest common denominator of Jewish life. It receives so much attention because it is public and secular. But it is not an alternative form of Jewish expression. This does not mean that it cannot or that it has not served as a vehicle to reintegrate an otherwise assimilating Jew into Jewish life. But this is true of only a small minority of Jews to whom I will return. To date, I am more impressed by the signs of erosion in support for Israel which bode poorly for the future.[22]

The third factor which helps account for the favorable assessment many make of American Jewish life derives from the misguided confidence they attribute to the results of survey research on American Jews. Survey research is an important instrument to assist our understanding of American Jewish life. But it is subject to certain inherent limitations and, of course, biases in interpretation to which, because of its scientific aura, the reader may not be alert.

Those who design questionnaires must choose a few questions from among a great number of possibilities. Furthermore, there is an advantage in repeating the same questions year after year in the same or different communities in order to facilitate comparisons. Unfortunately, the same question can be interpreted differently from one time period to the next, thereby providing misleading results.

A good example is the Passover *seder*. Many questionnaires ask respondents whether they attended a Passover *seder* at home or elsewhere during the past year. Around 85 percent of American Jews respond that they do. This, and results from similar type questions has lead Steven M.Cohen, the best known and one of the most thoughtful of the survey researchers to locate "the large majority of Jews . . . along the middle ranges of Jewish involvement."[23] In all fairness to Cohen, he does observe that "the quality of their Jewishness, the depth and significance of their affiliation, may leave much to be desired."[24] Furthermore, "middle range of Jewish involvement" is a relative term, although a reader may be tempted to forget this, particularly when he reads Cohen's policy conclusions. Cohen does use the Passover *seder* figure to demonstrate the continuity of Jewish loyalty to at least some ritual observance. The problem is that the term "Passover *seder*" can mean a family meal and little more to many American Jews. The anecdotal evidence points to the fact that when many American Jews report they attend a *seder* it doesn't mean they attend a ceremonial meal in which foods are prepared in accordance with Passover injunctions or that the Passover *haggadah*, the heart of the traditional Passover *seder*, is recited. We don't know how many American Jews celebrate the Passover *seder* in accordance with the Jewish tradition, however liberally one wishes to interpret that tradition, because survey researchers don't ask that question. The same is true for lighting Ḥanukkah or Sabbath candles. It is not inconceivable that the number of respondents who report that they engage in any of these activities may even be higher than the number who would have reported that they did so fifty years ago. But it is also likely that fifty years ago those who celebrated the Passover by sitting down to a family meal and nothing more would have realized that they were not in fact celebrating a *seder*.

A second problem is statistical interpretation. Is the glass half full or half empty? The answer depends in part on one's expectations. Lowered levels of expectation among obervers of contemporary Jewish life is further evidence, to me, of the erosion of Jewish life, not its continuing vigor. Cohen notes that 60 percent of Jewish couples with school age children are affiliated with a synagogue.[25] Cohen finds comfort in this figure though as he himself indicates and as every other survey of American Jews that asks the question confirms, the majority of Jews who affiliate with a synagogue do so when their children are of school age and disaffiliate after their youngest child reaches the age of 13. Rather than interpret this affiliation as a sign of continued Jewish commitment it seems to me more appropriate to label it as residual commitment. Jews still want a *bar* or *bat mitzvah* for their children and most of them probably want more than that.[26] They want their children to feel Jewish and since they are insecure about their ability to provide that feeling in the home they turn to synagogue sponsored schools to provide it.

Two additional problems with survey research of American Jews are the representativeness of the sample and the credibility of the responses. A Jew who explicitly denies his or her Jewishness will avoid the researchers net although the most traditional are lost as well. In addition, even someone who does not deny his past but who lives in a non-Jewish neighborhood, with no Jewish affiliations at all is less likely to fall into most samples. Survey researchers are aware of the problems and have been rather inventive in seeking to overcome them but the fact remains that the assimilated Jew is least likely to be tapped through survey research data.

Second, the respondents may exaggerate the degree of their Jewish behavior. This too, one might argue, is a positive sign. If respondents bother to lie about the intensity of their Jewish commitment it does suggest that they still care about demonstrating their Jewishness. But I am not arguing that the vast majority of American Jews are seeking to conceal their Jewish identity. That would be the final and not even necessary step in assimilating. The argument centers over the quality of their Jewishness and whether or not it is eroding. Hence, the accuracy of the figures are of significance. In Steven M.Cohen's 1986 National Survey of American Jews he finds that 61 percent report they fasted on Yom Kippur during the past year and 25 percent attended Sabbath services once a month or more during 1986. Neither figure is credible. Reform synagogues don't even hold services to the conclusion of Yom Kippur. Many of them end their services during the day with a repast of some kind. The figure of 61 percent suggests that respondents are either exaggerating their ritual performance or are defining a "fast" as fasting part of the day. The Sabbath attendance figure of 25 percent is no less incredulous. It would mean that synagogues are filled to capacity Sabbath after Sabbath.

Survey research is useful but it has its limits. It is unfortunate that Jewish sociologists have engaged in so little anthropological or ethnological type research which could speak to many of the questions raised here. Chaim Waxman has observed that most social scientists of American Jewry rely on demographic data and "have little grounding in either the sociology of religion or traditional Judaism, and they, therefore are oblivious to them."[27] I'm not sure that the matter stems from the lack of grounding in traditional Judaism but the absence of sensitivity to the sociology of religion is certainly true. I suspect it stems from a reluctance or inability of social scientists to provide a model of a community or a conception of Judaism against which they can assess American Jewish life. This may stem from a fear of the kinds of conclusions and policy implications such a model would offer.

The fourth factor contributing to a misconception about the success of American Jewish life is the fact that positive developments in one segment of the community are attributed to all American Jews. An estimated 12 percent of Jewish children between the ages of three and seventeen are enrolled in Jewish day schools. They constitute 28 percent of all Jewish children receiving some form of Jewish education. Although the figure drops to six percent by the final two years of high school it does mean that a minority, however small, of Jewish children receive a very intense form of Jewish education. This is a hopeful sign. The figures today are higher than they were in the past. But they hardly suggest that American Jews are becoming more intensely Jewish. Taken in conjunction with other developments they point to the fact that a minority of American Jews is seeking a more intense form of Jewish life.

Decisions by some Jews to dramatically alter their lives in a Jewish direction at the private religious level and/or the communal and organizational level are not unknown. Although most widely advertised as an Orthodox phenomenon it is not confined to the Orthodox. Deborah Lipstadt writes about young Jewish communal leaders who search for the meaning of their own Jewish sentiments:

> They are convinced that the nature of the communal work which they do has not only human but transcendental significance ... they exemplify the romantic strain which has emerged in American Jewish life and which seeks more than just a memory of Jewish life.[28]

There is a revival of Jewish life on college campuses. Some students with little background or interest in Judaism do suddenly find themselves interested and involved in Jewish activities and in discovering the meaning of being a Jew. Some academicians, previously indifferent and even contemptuous of Judaism are now engaged in a search to learn more of their own tradition. This search has become increasingly respectable as Judaism has gained in stature and importance in American culture. But it also reflects a sense of despair with the inchoate and rootless nature of modern culture which threatens one's sense of order in general and family stability in particular. This same phenomenon is found among young professionals who previously sought to ground their lives in their vocation and their professional associations but now find they require a more transcendent anchor in which they can root their sense of morality or derive an alternate system of values in their search for order.

The revival of Jewish life is reflected in the personal lives of many Jews as well as in the communal policies of Jewish organizations.[29] The American Jewish community is no longer led by those who seek to demonstrate that Jews are entitled to equal rights because Judaism is really no different than Christianity and entirely compatible with the values of middle-class America. Instead, Jewish leaders today are more concerned with the welfare of Jews in the United States, in Israel and elsewhere and in insuring the survival of American Judaism.

Jewish books of a serious nature, the translation and commentary upon traditional text, new interpretations of Jewish history, modern Jewish scholarship and belles lettres are all flourishing as never before in the American Jewish past. The list of books available from the *Jewish Bookshelf* published by B'nai B'rith is evidence of that.

These and other positive signs point to the possibility of an American Jewish revival. They demonstrate that Jewish life can flourish amid material prosperity and political freedom, that anti-semitism and suffering are not preconditions to Jewish loyalty. But they are not evidence of the positive identity and commitment of the vast majority of American Jews. Rather, they point to a polarization among American Jews and of the capacity of a minority to sustain and even strengthen their Jewish commitments despite the tendencies of the majority.

The phenomenon requires careful study. If we are to draw the appropriate policy implications we need to better understand those who affirm their Jewishness as well as those who seek to escape it.

I think that observers of American Jewish life, social scientists in particular have fallen into a trap innocently laid by an earlier generation of rabbis, educators and some social scientists as well. When those Jews talked about Jewish survival, it was not the threat of biological disappearance which troubled them. After all, the key term in their vocabulary was "assimilation" not "extinction." The demographers may have been troubled by birthrate projections but the discussion of Jewish survival was in the context of whether substantial numbers of Jews would remain committed to Judaism, i.e. to a Jewish tradition however one defined it; to a set of conceptions, beliefs and practices that were meaningfully related to the conceptions, beliefs and practices associated with the Jewish past. Those who ruminated about Jewish survival were concerned with whether American Jews would find images of themselves reproduced in the future, not whether there would be a biological or genetic link between Jews of the present and future generations. The language in which these concerns were expressed was the language of survival. That was a big mistake. When intermarriage and birthrate figures suggested the risk of biological attrition Jewish spokesmen seized upon this data. I suppose they hoped that this would alarm the vast majority of Jews. American Jews had accepted the decline in the quality of Jewish life, the attenuation of the ties between the lives Jews lead and the lives Jews led in the past, the lowered intensity of Jewish commitment with equanimity. I suppose that Jewish spokesmen hoped that the fear of no grandchildren or of grandchildren who were not Jewish would arouse American Jews from their lethargy.

Those who raised the alarm about biological extinction were factually incorrect. The data on mixed marriages is alarming. But there is a segment of the Jewish community, certainly the Orthodox but others as well, who are concerned with and committed to Judaism and they show no signs of disappearing. But much of what I read by the optimists of Jewish life is not about these Jews. Much of the literature addresses itself to the alarmist or biological argument which is not or ought not to be the core concern of

Jewish communal leaders. These concerns, as I already suggested, are not readily addressed by quantitative data. At the very least they require a more careful structuring of questionnaires, more personal interviews, more participant-observation, greater attentiveness to cultural artifacts; in short more anthropological type studies of greater historical sensitivity. The recent message of American Jewish sociologists has been don't worry, alarmist projections are wrong, Jews aren't disappearing. This message, I fear, is then decoded to mean that American Judaism is prospering. If that is what American Jewish sociologists mean I can only say "God protects the foolish." But if what American Jewish sociologists really mean, and this is what some of them tell me, is that the quality of Jewish life is terrible but Jews will survive biologically, then they ought to formulate their message more carefully or they bear the charge of irresponsibility.

Notes

1. Charles Liebman, "Jewish Accommodation to America: A Reappraisal," *Commentary* 64 (August 1977):57–60.
2. Charles Liebman, "Leadership and Decision Making In a Jewish Community: The New York Federation of Jewish Philanthropies," *American Jewish Year Book, 1979* (Philadelphia:Jewish Publication Society, 1979), pp.3–76.
3. I don't mean to suggest that wife abuse is the moral equivalent of mixed marriage. I would rather that my son marry a non-Jew than batter his wife. But given current standards of morality I had some difficulty in identifying a form of behavior which is almost universally condemned in American society.
4. Bruce Phillips, *Border Cities: Three Jewish Communities in the American West* (forthcoming).
5. *Trends*, 11 (Spring 1986). *Trends* is a newsletter published by the Jewish Education Service of North America (JESNA) for Federation leaders.
6. In all fairness, a forthcoming study on rabbinical students at the Jewish Theological Seminary and its various branches indicates that Judaica courses in college were an important factor in decisions to attend rabbinical school. The article, however, reenforces my next major point. The authors find that students were not influenced by the Conservative movement's own socializing institutions (its camps and youth movements) in their decision. Aryeh Davidson and Jack Wertheimer, "The Next Generation of Conservative Rabbis: An Empirical Study of Today's Rabbinical Students," *American Jewish Year Book 1987* (forthcoming).
7. I tried to make this point in chapter one. See also, Steven M. Cohen, *American Modernity and Jewish Identity* (New York: Tavistock, 1983).
8. Roselyn Bell, "Houston," *Hadassah Magazine* (October 1986):30.
9. *The Jewish Floridian*, (6 November 1986).
10. *Connecticut Jewish Ledger* (6 and 13 November 1986).
11. A very helpful discussion of this phenomenon is found in Milton Gordon's chapter 'The Nature of Assimilation" in his book *Assimilation in American Life* (New York: Oxford University Press, 1964), pp. 60–83. I am not suggesting

that American Jews have followed the pattern of assimilation which Gordon suggests. They have not.

12. See, for example, his statement in *Will There be One Jewish People By the Year 2000?* (New York: The National Jewish Center for Learning and Leadership, "Critical Issues Conference," March 16–17 1986), pp.42–52.

13. Schindler's explanation of the Reform movement's decision begins with the statement that "Reform is unalterably opposed to intermarriage, even as are the Orthodox and Conservative religious communities . . . we resist intermarriage with every resource at our command." (Ibid., pp. 47–48.) Someone like myself, who questions the accuracy of that statement is led to believe that it was offered to convince non-Reform representatives of Reform's noble intentions. Thus, it seems reasonable to me to conclude that when Schindler formulates his defense of the patrilineal descent decision in terms of the Jewish tradition or the requirements of Jewish survival he is offering this defense as an apology rather than a sincerely held conviction.

14. Calvin Goldscheider and Alan Zuckerman, *The Transformation of the Jews* (Chicago: University of Chicago Press, 1984).

15. *Connecticut Jewish Ledger* (31 July 1986):2.

16. Ibid.,(7 August 1986):2.

17. Charles Silberman, *A Certain People* (New York: Summit Books, 1985).

18. Dan Oren, *Joining the Club: A History of Jews and Yale* (New Haven: Yale University Press, 1985), 18.

19. David Lodge, *Changing Places* (London: Martin Secker and Warburg, 1975).

20. Calvin Goldscheider, *Jewish Continuity and Change* (Bloomington: Indiana University Press, 1986), p. 152.

21. Cohen, p.156.

22. See, for example, Steven M.Cohen's 1986 Survey of American Jews presented to the Association of Jewish Studies meetings in Boston, December 14–16, 1986. In the discussion which followed Cohen's presentation some members of the audience noted that these findings confirmed their own observations.

23. Steven M. Cohen, "Outreach to the Marginally Affiliated: Evidence and Implication for Policymakers in Jewish Education," *Journal of Jewish Communal Service*, 62 (Winter 1985):149.

24. Ibid.

25. Ibid., p. 148.

26. The widespread celebration of the *bat mitzvah* service (the equivalent for girls of the *bar mitzvah* service for boys) in Conservative as well as Reform synagogues has probably resulted in lengthening the period during which parents remain affiliated to a synagogue.

27. Chaim Waxman, "The Limits of Futurology: Conflicting Perspectives on the American Jewish Community," in *Survey of Jewish Affairs, 1986* ed. William Frankel (forthcoming).

28. Deborah Lipstadt, "From Noblesse Oblige to Personal Redemption: The Changing Profile and Agenda of American Jewish Leaders," *Modern Judaism*, 4 (October 1984):304–305.

29. Liebman, "Leadership and Decision Making . . . ," describes the impact of these changes on the policies of the New York Federation of Jewish Philanthropies.

7

Reflections on Social Science and Jewish Public Policy

I made a number of references in chapters five and six to the policy consequences or implications of the transformationist and traditionalist approaches. But I remained somewhat vague about the specific nature of these policies. I have never felt very comfortable with exploring the relationship between social science research or analysis and its policy implications. I am not very good at it and perhaps because I am not good at it I'm not especially interested in the topic. I don't mean to suggest that I don't consider the topic an important one. I do. Hence, I am consoled by the fact that there is such a lively interest in the topic and so many other social scientists are prepared to carry the banner of policy studies.

My own inclinations which lead me to shy away from such studies are reenforced by my suspicion that, at least in the social sciences, the relationship between policy and research is not as firm as is often supposed. In a recent essay Christopher Jencks has put the matter as sharply as I would dare to do:

> Social science is restricted to the study of the past. Worse yet, rigorous social science is restricted to studying those aspects of the past that have been recorded in fairly consistent categories, like births, marriages, votes, tax rates, and murders. It can never hope to achieve much rigor in studying the subjective meanings that people attach to events, even though these meanings are critical to understanding why things happened as they did and what is likely to happen in the future. As a result, those who want to remake society can never hope to get reliable advice from social scientists. Incremental reformers may get some hints, but even they must look elsewhere most of the time.[1]

Jencks' statement alone ought to serve as fair warning to the Jewish communal leaders who increasingly press Jewish social scientists to outline

95

the policy consequences of their research. But I want to elaborate on the warning by first offering some general observations and then citing some specific examples from Jewish life.

First of all, social science's predictive capacity is minimal. Indeed, the question self respecting social scientists ought to ask is why do governments, foundations and other institutions and organizations keep turning to them for advice and journalists quote them at length given their abysmal track record. The answer is probably related to the reassurance with which social science provides us that the world is not chaotic or random; that events occur in accordance with some laws, that everything has a cause, that this cause is not only definable (knowable) but even controllable. One cannot help but recall that this bears a remarkable resemblance to the functions which sociologists of religion attribute to religion. Apparently, at least part of the reason for the attraction of each is that they not only promise salvation (each in their own way) but reassure us in matters that evoke our deepest anxieties. But those concerned with actually changing reality rather than finding reassurance about the nature of reality will find that social science is a frail instrument indeed. Although some of its leading practitioners may speak with a voice of confidence and certainty, the fact is that their analyses of reality, whether it be economic, social or political and their prescriptions for the future keep changing. I sometimes think that the greatest compliment one can pay to social scientists is to observe that many of them will at least readjust their theories and analyses after events have proven them wrong or misguided, though it often takes long enough for them to do this. A few, of course, refuse to acknowledge any inconsistency between their theory and reality and continue to distort their descriptions of reality by seeking to impose their conceptions upon it. There is no better example than the one I have referred to at a number of places in this volume: modernization theory. Modernization, we once all believed, was a package combining urbanization, industrialization, increased education and other factors which lead inevitably to economic growth, political mobilization, democracy, secularization (the decline of religious belief and practice), the strengthening of national (i.e.statist) identity at the expense of an ethnic one and eventually to the imposition of an international identity at the expense of a national one. It is questionable whether the package called modernization really exists; or, more properly, whether the conception is a very useful one when generalizing about all societies. There is certainly nothing inevitable about it. Nor, in those societies which have experinced economic growth, urbanization and higher levels of educational attainment has there always been an increase in secularization or a stronger national and weaker ethnic identity. This is of consequence to those concerned with Jewish public policy, especially policies dealing with assimilation because modernization theory has been an important component in many analyses of Jewish life. Some social scientists continue to tinker with modernization theory. Some of them now seek to explain why it results in exactly the opposite consequences which were earlier predicted.[2] Jewish policymakers are better advised to turn their attention to a lower order level of concepts.

Secondly, the policymaking enterprise is constrained by the unspoken assumptions and built in agendas of the policymakers themselves. My argument is that when social science analysis leads to policy implications contrary to the implicit values or beliefs of the policymakers they are likely to reject the analysis. For example, Jewish organizational leaders are explicitly committed to the values of Jewish survival or strengthening Jewish life in the United States. Let us assume, for the sake of argument, that I could make a strong case, convincing to non-partisan observers, that strict separation of religion and state in the manner urged by such groups as the American Civil Liberties Union and most Jewish organizations (the American Jewish Congress in particular) erodes Jewish life. I don't believe that this would have any impact on American Jewish attitudes toward religion and state any more than demonstrating that Jews were assimilating in the United States and that such assimilation was inevitable (an argument I do not believe can be made) and would lead to increased *aliyah*. This doesn't mean that American Jewish leaders aren't committed to strengthening Jewish life. It means that they have other values as well and these values lead to the rejection of any counsel that forces them to choose between these values. What, one supposes, the policymakers would do if they were also committed to the ideal of research and analyses is shop around to find the right social scientist or the right analyses whose policy implications suit their proclivities. Given the tenuous nature of social science analyses this is not very difficult to do.

This leaves us with the limited audiences to whom social science analysis is useful. It is an audience which shares a whole series of values and is prepared to consult the social scientist on appropriate strategies to affect these values. Can the social scientist be of help? Maybe. For example, the consultant may chart the parameters of the feasible. But then again, he/she may not. During the 1970s Jewish organizations spent time and money in sponsoring conferences and research on how Jewish birthrates could be increased. Sometimes in tandem and more often independently, Jewish organizations also sought to explore ways to reduce the number of Jews marrying non-Jews (mixed marriage). Many social scientists don't believe there is anything the Jewish community can do about raising birthrates or reducing mixed marriage rates. The Jewish community found such counsel unsatisfactory and turned to social scientists who were prepared to urge one strategy or another. Finally, despairing of organizational strategies to raise birthrates or reduce mixed marriage rates and unwilling to live with the frustrating sense that the Jewish community was in trouble and nothing can be done about it many Jewish leaders embraced a new type of analysis in the 1980s; the analysis that argued that there was nothing to fear from low birthrates or a high incidence of mixed marriage.

But there is also a danger in accepting the counsel of social scientists about the limits of the feasible. People respond to symbols and perception, not to the reality of an environment. Christopher Jencks noted that this is the area about which social scientists can tell us the least. Furthermore, they are likely to couch their advice in terms of "other things remaining equal" which is never true. By assuming a controlled environment social science underestimates the possibilities which new conditions offer. I can think of no better example than the feasibility of establishing a Jewish state as it must have appeared in the 1930s and 1940s. I don't believe that any objective and intelligent social scientist would have counseled Jewish groups to continue their efforts on behalf of a Jewish state. Jews would be better advised, an objective social scientist would have said, to invest their efforts and energies in other directions.

The previous discussion raises another set of questions. If policy can only emerge in the presence of value consensus how do Jewish leaders make policy? Is there really a consensus among them about the nature of Judaism and Jewish values? One answer is that the question misinterprets how Jewish policy is actually formulated in the United States. It is not necessarily a product of any deliberative body of people, it is not even the product of any single person's attention to policy consequences; rather it is an outcome of what many different individual Jews and many different Jewish organizations do. Policy, in other words, is not a category of decision making but rather a name associated with the end result of many intended and unintended activities. This is not only true of Jews. It is true of institutions and communities which have far greater resources and coercive powers at their disposal. It is true of governments including that of the United States. But it also underestimates the degree of organization and planning that is found in at least some organizations and in some communities. The Federations of Jewish Philanthropies at the local and national level are one such example. Not everything they do is thoughtful, well planned or effectively executed. But it would be a gross diminution of the seriousness of their enterprise or that of organizations such as the American Jewish Committee or the Anti-Defamation League or the American Jewish Congress to think that they do not give serious consideration to policymaking. Hence the question remains: how can they do so in the absence of value consensus? What they have done is bypass the question by articulating a set of values which are minimal enough and vague enough to provide a basis for common discourse and to which appeal can be made for ultimate legitimation of policy. This is particularly appropriate where policies are enunciated at a general level and left to professionals to implement. The policy execution side of Jewish life has received very little attention. We don't have any studies which have addressed themselves to the broad question.[3] On the other hand, a recent study by Jonathan Woocher explores value consensus among Federation leaders.[4] Woocher points to the remarkable success of Federation leaders in formulating what he labels Jewish civil religion which embraces not only values but a set of myths and rituals that both legitimate and reinforce these values. Not surprisingly, however, the values, vague to begin with, are least specific in reference to Judaism and more specific about the interests of American Jews. Jewish communal leaders are able to articulate needs which presumably affect all Jews and which can be achieved through fundraising or political means but which avoid encroaching on the private behavior of Jews. Jewish leaders are most comfortable when they can justify some program by appealing to instrumental interests couched ultimately in the vague language of Jewish survival. They are least comfortable with, indeed they resist formulating policies and programs that point to or emanate from conceptions of Judaism.

Mixed marriage and Jewish education are two such examples. As I indicated in the previous chapter, objection to mixed marriage or support for Jewish education are justified not because one is intrinsically wrong and the other intrinsically right but because of their ostensible effect on Jewish survival or Jewish identity. This, however, is a problematic basis for justifying a program unless one has a conception about what Jewish survival or Jewish identity means; that is unless one has a vision of what it means to live a Jewish life. Such a vision, however, has less to do with politics or the material interests of Jews (the kinds of activities and programs which Jewish leaders prefer to engage in) and a great deal to do with how one conducts one's own Jewish life (the kinds of issues which Jewish leaders prefer to avoid). Despite all the discussion that went on in the 1970s over the needs to raise Jewish birth rates or prevent mixed marriages, no Jewish organization resolved that its own members or officers should be urged to have more children or be ruled ineligible for office if they supported planned parenthood societies or married outside the faith. Some organizations do have rules with regard to mixed marriage but none adopted them in response to the crises which presumably confronted American Jews in the 1970s. The State of Israel and the Holocaust, as Woocher points out, are the crucial symbols of the civil religion. At least part of the reason, in my opinion, rests on the fact that these two symbols point to that which American Jews (leaders in particular) want to do and makes no demands upon them in areas they wish to avoid. Israel reminds American Jews of the need to organize for and expend enormous effort on political activity. The Holocaust legitimates vigilance against the threat of anti-semitism, however vague the threat may appear at any given time. This creates an insider-outsider syndrome and reduces the significance of internal differences among Jews. The challenge, the Holocaust memory suggests, comes from outside the Jewish people and threatens all Jews alike; therefore, we have a firm bases for unity; the manner in which one lives one's private life is of no consequence.

I have no quarrel with the importance of the State of Israel, no argument with the fact that real enemies threaten its existence and the need for American Jews to organize in its support. I also believe that the victims of the Holocaust should be commemorated and the events of the Holocaust remembered. But neither the State of Israel, much less the Holocaust are core components much less the major content of Judaism as I understand Judaism. American Jews have minimized *Judaism* and substituted the defense of Jewish interests or Jewishness or ethnic Judaism, call it what you will, as their chief matters of concern. Judaism, what one believes about God and Torah, has become secondary to Jewishness, how one defines and defends the interest of the Jewish people. This is paradoxical because the two are interrelated. But that may be more true among the masses of Jews than among the leaders themselves. Jewish policymakers have been inclined to separate them. Such efforts are understandable. They make consensus building easier and preserve unity. But they are ultimately mistaken. Perhaps a better way of putting it is that they have gone too far; a point to which I will return.

Judaism and Jewishness are interrelated as I already indicated in the behavior of most American Jews. I noted a number of times in earlier chapters that public concern for Jewish interests is not an alternative to involvement in the synagogue or ritual observance. Rather, the two forms of behavior are correlated. As the most recently published study concludes with regard to voluntary association activity, "religious activity is the main gateway to further involvement."[5]

This should not surprise us. A deep level of commitment to ethnic Judaism or the defense of Jewish interests is not self legitimating, least of all in the present period in the United States. Unless one is committed to Judaism as a religion its public aspects are unlikely to evoke any special resonance. This is not true in Israel and it was not true in Europe until recently. There, threats to the material welfare of the Jewish people could have evoked an ethnic sentiment devoid of a religious basis. But why should American Jews involve themselves in Jewish life in the United

States if they have no commitment to Judaism? The threats to Israel are not really imminent and it remains in the American national interest to defend Israel's survival anyway; the plight of Soviet Jewry pales in comparison to the suffering of large numbers of other people throughout the world. On a universal scale of human fear, suffering and oppression, no group of Jews anywhere in the world, with the exception of Ethiopean Jewry has a particularly high priority.

Furthermore, we ought not to confuse Jewish concerns with all of the current Jewish involvement in American politics. Politics has became the most glamorous of Jewish activity in recent years. Jews contribute enormous sums to political candidates. Such contributions do not necessarily serve the interest of the Jewish people, never mind that they have nothing to do with Judaism. I don't fault the contributors on these grounds. Individuals have the right to spend their money as they see fit. But it is my observation that increasing numbers of Jews contribute funds to political campaigns under the pretense that in so doing they are furthering Jewish interests. This pretension deserves to be challenged. It is my impression that political contributions have become the newest game for wealthy Jews, a game sometimes carried on without regard to its consequences for Jewish interests.

I do not recommend that Jews abandon their involvement in politics. I certainly do not suggest that Jewish organizations no longer concern themselves with the material interests of the Jewish people. I do urge that such activities be viewed in context and that in adopting "policy," Jewish organizations not confine themselves exclusively or even primarily to Jewish material concerns.

I have no principled solution to a problem of whose dimensions I am aware. The public-political realm merits attention. Secondly, if Jewish organizations are to adopt stands or take action affecting the private lives of Jews, i.e. Judaism, they may engender disharmony. This also means that many policies that I view as critical will not be undertaken by national or roof organizations but by smaller or local or more issue-oriented groups who share a wider value consensus among their members. I do not have a specific program to present to national Jewish organizations or leaders. Each has their own set of problems and their own internal agendas and priorities that make it difficult for them to adopt positions in areas that I consider central to Judaism and therefore critical to Jewish life. Obviously it would be difficult for the American Jewish Committee or the Council of Jewish Federations and Welfare Funds to condemn the recent decision by Reform rabbis to recognize the children of Jewish fathers and non-Jewish mothers as Jews. I think that decision is a disaster for Judaism and is more threatening to American Jewish life than any anti-semitic movement in the

United States. But even if a majority could be mustered within such organizations to condemn the Reform decision it would surely antagonize many of their leading members and contributors. I think that observing dietary laws is a far more central component of Judaism than, for example, supporting Jewish hospitals; even when those hospitals are located in Israel. But I am aware of the difficulty Jewish organizations would have if they sought to devote even a small part of their energies to increasing observance of dietary laws among American Jews. The fact is that since most American Jews do not observe such laws we may reasonably guess that neither do many leaders of these same organizations whom I am urging to encourage it. There is, therefore, a rationale to the informal division of labor in Jewish organizational life which leaves concern for Judaism in the hands of the religious denominational groups whereas the "secular" Jewish organizations devote themselves to issues concerning Jewish material welfare. But both sides would deny that such a division is feasible. The "secular" Jewish organizations, the large voluntary organizations which are the real powers and movers in Jewish life today would certainly deny that they are not concerned with Judaism. They even take umbrage at the term "secular" preferring to label themselves "non-denominational." The "religious" or "denominational" organizations are aware of the fact that any conception of Judaism incorporates a public dimension and a concern for Jewish material interests. Nevertheless, there is a division of labor which I do not hope nor would I want to entirely erase. I am simply urging a different balance of concerns. In an imperfect world I have despaired of ideal solutions. Jewish leaders, I am arguing, have gone too far in seeking to further the material interests of Jews while neglecting Judaism and the requirements of Judaism. Let them at least acknowledge this. Then let them take account of the organizational constraints that impose difficulties in this regard. But do not make a virtue of what is at most an unfortunate necessity.

This argument proceeds from an assumption that there is such a thing as Judaism with its own essence and to be a good Jew means living one's life in accordance with the precepts of Judaism; that whatever specific mission a Jewish organization assigns to itself, its ultimate objective is promoting and strengthening Judaism; that not everything Jews do is authentically Jewish or Judaic even when done in the company of other Jews and for the sake of what they call Judaism.

This may seem like a remarkably bland incontrovertible statement. But it is not only contrary to what the more extreme transformationists (see chapter five) would affirm. It is also contrary to expressions of opinion which I increasingly hear and read. *Moment* magazine, under the editorship of Leonard Fein (he sold the magazine in 1987) was the most popular and probably the most influential Jewish publication in Jewish leadership circles. Here is what Fein had to say on the subject:

> Every generation of Jews, since the very beginning, has had its own interpreting to do, and has made its own mistakes. Authenticity requires not imitation, but interpretation—that more than anything else, is the authentic mandate.[6]

I completely agree with this statement. Judaism must evolve. That is not only a requisite for survival but my own precondition for commitment. I have no interest in remaining a Jew if Judaism denies my right to contribute of myself to its evolution. But Fein goes on to say something immediately thereafter which I find most insidious.

> In truth, I want to say something more here. I want to say that we, the living Jews of this generation, *are* the text, as our grandparents were in their day and as our grandchildren will be, God willing in theirs."(emphasis in the original)[7]

This statement, its elegance and invocation of God to the contrary notwithstanding, is historically inaccurate and normatively disastrous. Jews for Jesus, the Black Hebrews, Brother Daniel (the Carmelite monk who sought citizenship in Israel as a Jew) and indeed the whole Christian church all argued that they were/are the living Jews of their generation. We deny their claim based on the absence of fidelity on their part to what we claim is the authentic tradition. Remove the conception of tradition, deny the argument that there is a Judaism, affirm the right of Jews to formulate Judaism as they see fit without regard to the past and there is no basis for argument with anyone's Jewish claim.

Throughout this book I have cited evidence that Orthodox Jews are better Jews (not necessarily better human beings) than the non-Orthodox by any reasonable measure of Jewish commitment. Why is this true? I do not attribute any magical quality to ritual observance. But the observance of Jewish ritual is the most effective instrument we know to locate the Jew in a culture and traditon. At the present time, in the United States, there is no substitute for ritual in integrating a Jew into Jewish culture and conveying the sense of a common past and future.

The language and culture which American Jews share seem to me to be less and less Jewish. It is, at most, American Jewishness whose ties to the past are becoming increasingly attenuated. The past is becoming either trivial or irrelevant to American Jews. Their ties to other communities, it seems to me, are increasingly sustained not by a real sense of community but by slogans that are proving increasingly fragile.

I am suggesting, therefore, that Jewish policymakers must concern themselves with Judaism as well as with Jews and their policies must be authentically Jewish; that is faithful to the tradition. This does not mean that only scholars or rabbis can be policymakers. It does mean that since policies are subject to the test of the tradition, those most knowledgeable of the tradition must make their voices heard. This, in turn, may mean that scholars and rabbis will have to be better trained to understand Jewish policy in order to participate effectively in its determination. But the ideal is not a division of labor between, for example, lay leaders who make policy and masters of the tradition who have some approval or veto power. The ideal is to sensitize all Jews or at least all Jewish leaders to the tradition. This means not only study of Jewish sources and experiencing Jewish life in a traditional setting (such programs already exist for training of lay leaders) it also means that individuals who lack sensitivity to the tradition forfeit their right to hold Jewish public office.

Notes

1. *New York Review* (11 June 1987):52.
2. See, for example, Anthony Smith, *The Ethnic Revival* (Cambridge: Cambridge University Press, 1981) or Katherine O'Sullivan See, *First World Nationalisms* (Chicago: University of Chicago Press, 1986) and the literature cited therein.
3. One study that deals with the inputs of policy formation in a particular context is Steven M.Cohen, "Israeli Emigres and the New York Federation: A Case Study in Ambivalent Policymaking for 'Jewish Communal Deviants'" in *Contemporary Jewry 7* Arnold Dashefsky, editor (New Brunswick, N.J.: Transaction Books, 1986):155–165. I also try to deal with the question in my study "Leadership and Decision Making in a Jewish Community: The New York Federation of Jewish Philanthropies" *American Jewish Year Book 1979* (Philadelphia: Jewish Publication Society, 1979), pp. 3–76. See also, Daniel Elazar, *Community and Polity: The Organizational Dynamics of American Jewry* (Philadelphia: Jewish Publication Society, 1976).
4. Jonathan Woocher, *Sacred Survival: The Civil Religion of American Jews* (Bloomington: Indiana University Press, 1986).
5. Alan York and Bernard Lazerwitz, "Religious Involvement as the Main Gateway to Voluntary Association Activity," in *Contemporary Jewry 8* Arnold Dashefsky, editor (New Brunswick, N.J.: Transaction Books, 1987), p. 23.
6. Leonard Fein, "We are the Text," *Moment* 21 (March 1987):39.
7. Ibid.

Bibliography

Argyle, Michael, and Beit-Hallahmi, Benjamin, *The Social Psychology of Religion*, (London: Routledge and Kegan Paul,1975).

Bell, Daniel, "Return of the Sacred? The Argument on the Future of Religion," *British Journal of Sociology*, 38 (December 1977), 419–449.

Bell, Roselyn, "Houston," *Hadassah Magazine*, October 1986.

Bellah, Robert N., *Beyond Belief*, (New York: Harper and Row, 1970).

Bensimon-Donat, Doris, "North African Jews in France," *Dispersion and Unity*, 10 (Winter 1970), 119–135.

Berger, Brigitte and Peter, "Our Conservatism and Theirs," *Commentary*, 82 (October 1986), 62–67.

Berger, Peter, *The Heretical Imperative*, (Garden City, N.Y.:Doubleday, Anchor Books, 1979).

Berger, Peter, *The Sacred Canopy*, (Garden City, N.Y.: Doubleday, Anchor Books, 1969).

Bibby, Reginald, "Why Conservative Churches *Really* Are Growing: Kelley Revisited," *Journal for the Scientific Study of Religion*, 17 (June 1978), 129–137.

Bocock, Robert, *Ritual in Industrial Society*, (London: George Allen and Unwin, 1974).

Caplovitz, David, and Sherrow, Fred, *The Religious Drop-Outs: Apostasy Among College Graduates*, (Beverly Hills: Sage,1977).

Cohen, Steven M., "Will Jews Keep Giving? Prospects for the Jewish Charitable Community," *Journal of Jewish Communal Service*, 55 (Autumn 1978), 59–71.

Cohen, Steven M., *American Modernity and Jewish Identity*, (New York: Tavistock, 1983).

Cohen, Steven M., "Outreach to the Marginally Affiliated: Evidence and Implications for Policymakers in Jewish Education," *Journal of Jewish Communal Service*, 62 (Winter 1985).

Cohen, Steven M., "Israeli Emigres and the New York Federation: A Case Study in Ambivalent Policymaking for 'Jewish Communal Deviants,'" *Contemporary Jewry*, 7, (New Brunswick, N.J.: Transaction Books, 1986).

Cohen, Steven M., *Ties and Tensions: The 1986 Survey of American Jewish Attitudes Toward Israel and Israelis*, (New York:American Jewish Committee, 1987).

Cohen, Steven M., and Fein, Leonard, "From Integration to Survival: American Jewish Anxieties in Transition," *Annals of the American Association of Social and Political Science*, 480 (1985), 91–102.

Creevey, Lucy, "Religion and Modernization in Senegal," *Islam and Political Development*, John Esposito, ed., (Syracuse: Syracuse University Press, 1980).

Danziger, Shlomo, "Jewish Action Symposium," *Jewish Action*, 46 (1986).

Davidson, Aryeh, and Wertheimer, Jack, "The Next Generation of Conservative Rabbis: An Empirical Study of Today's Rabbinical Students," *American Jewish Year Book 1987*, (Philadelphia: Jewish Publication Society, 1987).

Deshen, Shlomo, "The Judaism of Middle Eastern Immigrants," *The Jerusalem Quarterly*, no. 13 (Fall 1979), 89–110.

Douglas, Mary, *Natural Symbols*, (New York: Random House, Vintage Books, 1973).

Douglas, Mary, *Purity and Danger*, (London: Routledge and Kegan Paul, 1966).

Ducey, Michael H., *Sunday Morning: Aspects of Urban Ritual*, (New York: The Free Press, 1977).

Elazar, Daniel, *Community and Polity: The Organizational Dynamics of American Jewry*, (Philadelphia: Jewish Publication Society, 1976).

Elazar, Daniel, "The Kehilla: From Its Beginning to the End of the Modern Epoch," *Public Life in Israel and the Diaspora*, Sam Lehman-Wilzig and Bernard Susser, eds., (Ramat-Gan,Israel: Bar-Ilan University Press, 1981).

Eliade, Mircea, "Myths, Dreams and Mysteries: The Encounter Between Contemporary Faiths and Archaic Realities," Reprinted in *Myth and Symbol*, F.W. Dillistone, ed., (London: S.P.C.K., 1966).

Eliade, Mircea, *The Sacred and the Profane*, (New York: Harcourt Brace and World, 1959).

Ellenson, David, "Rabbi Esriel Hildesheimer and the Quest for Religious Authority," *Modern Judaism*, 1 (September 1981), 279-297.

Fein, Leonard, "We Are the Text," *Moment*, 21 (March 1987).

Friedman, Menachem, "Haredim Confront the Modern City," *Studies in Contemporary Jewry*, 2, (Bloomington: Indiana University Press, 1986).

Friedman, Menachem, "Life Tradition and Book Tradition in the Development of Ultraorthodox Judaism," *Judaism Viewed From Within and From Without*, Harvey Goldberg, ed., (Albany: State University of New York, 1987), 235–255.

Geertz, Clifford, "Religion as a Cultural System," Clifford Geertz, *The Interpretation of Cultures*, (New York: Basic Books, 1973).

Geertz, Clifford, *Islam Observed*, (New Haven: Yale University Press, 1968).

Glazer, Nathan, *American Judaism*, (Chicago: University of Chicago Press, 1957).

Glazer, Nathan, *New Perspectives in American Jewish Sociology*, (New York: American Jewish Committee, 1987).

Glazer, Nathan, and Moynihan, Daniel, *Beyond the Melting Pot*, (Cambridge, MA: The M.I.T. Press, 1963).

Glick, Leonard, "The Anthropology of Religion: Malinowski and Beyond," *Essays in the Scientific Study of Religion*, Charles Glock and Phillip E. Hammond, eds., (New York: Harper and Row, 1973).

Glock, Charles Y., and Bellah, Robert N., eds., *The New Religious Consciousness*, (Berkeley: The University of California Press, 1976).

Glock, Charles Y., and Hammond, Phillip E., eds., *Beyond the Classics: Essays in the Scientific Study of Religion*, (New York: Harper and Row, 1973).

Goldman, Eliezer, "Responses to Modernity in Orthodox Jewish Thought," *Studies in Contemporary Jewry*, 2, (Bloomington: Indiana University Press, 1986).

Goldscheider, Calvin, *Jewish Continuity and Change*, (Bloomington:Indiana University Press, 1986).

Goldscheider, Calvin, and Zuckerman, Alan, *The Transformation of the Jews*, (Chicago: University of Chicago Press, 1984).

Gordon, Milton, *Assimilation in American Life*, (New York: Oxford University Press, 1964).

Greeley, Andrew, *Unsecular Man*, (New York: Schocken Books, 1975).

Harrison, Paul M., *Authority and Power in the Free Church Tradition*, (Princeton: Princeton University Press, 1959).

Hay, David, and Morisy, Ann, "Reports of Ecstatic, Paranormal or Religious Experience in Great Britain and the United States—a Comparison of Trends," *Journal for the Scientific Study of Religion*, 17 (September 1978), 255–68.

Heilman, Sam and Cohen, Steven M., "Ritual Variations Among Modern Orthodox Jews in the United States," *Studies in Contemporary Jewry*, 2, (Bloomington: Indiana University Press, 1986).

Herman, Simon, *Jewish Identity: A Social Psychological Perspective*, (Beverly Hills: Sage, 1977).

Hill, Michael, *A Sociology of Religion*, (London: Heinemann, 1973).

Himmelfarb, Harold S., "Patterns of Assimilation-Identification Among American Jews," Paper presented to the Seventh World Congress of Jewish Studies, Jerusalem, 1977.

Katz, Jacob, *Tradition and Crises*, (New York: The Free Press, 1969).

Katz, Jacob, *Out of the Ghetto; The Social Background of Jewish Emancipation 1770–1870*, (Cambridge, Mass.: Harvard University Press, 1973).

Kelley, Dean M., *Why Conservative Churches are Growing*, (New York: Harper and Row, 1972).

Knaani, David, *HaBatim Shehayu: Studies in History of the Jewish Family*, (Tel Aviv: Sifriat Poalim, in Hebrew, 1986).

Lazerwitz, Bernard, "Religious Identification and its Ethnic Correlates," *Social Forces*, 52 (December 1973), 204–22.

Lazerwitz, Bernard, "An Approach to the Components and Consequences of Jewish Identification," *Contemporary Jewry*, 4, (New Brunswick, N.J.: Transaction Books, 1978).

Lazerwitz, Bernard, "Some Jewish Reactions to the Six Day War," *Reconstructionist*, 34, November 8, 1967.

Lazerwitz, Bernard, and Harrison, Michael, "American Jewish Denominations: A Social and Religious Profile," *American Sociological Review*, 44 (August 1979), 656–66.

Leach, Edmund, *Genesis As Myth*, (London: Jonathan Cape, 1969).

Lenski, Gerhard, *The Religious Factor*, (Garden City, N.Y.: Doubleday, 1961).

Levi-Strauss, Claude, "The Structured Study of Myth," Reprinted in *Reader in Comparative Religion*, William Lessa and Evan Vogt, eds., (New York: Harper and Row, second ed., 1965).

Liebman, Charles S., "Orthodoxy in American Jewish Life," *American Jewish Year Book 1965*, (Philadelphia: Jewish Publication Society, 1965).

Liebman, Charles S., "Changing Social Characteristics of Orthodox, Conservative and Reform Jews," *Sociological Analysis*, 27 (Winter 1966), 210–22.

Liebman, Charles S., *The Ambivalent American Jew*, (Philadelphia: Jewish Publication Society, 1973).

Liebman, Charles S., "American Jewry: Identity and Affiliation," *The Future of the Jewish Community in America*, David Sidorsky, ed., (New York: Basic Books, 1973)4.

Liebman, Charles S., "Jewish Accommodation to America: A Reappraisal," *Commentary*, 64 (August 1977), 57–60.

Liebman, Charles S., "Myth, Tradition and Values in Israeli Society," *Midstream*, 24 (January 1978), 44–53.

Liebman, Charles S., "Leadership and Decision Making in a Jewish Community: The New York Federation of Jewish Philanthropies," *American Jewish Year Book 1979*, (Philadelphia: Jewish Publication Society, 1979).

Liebman, Charles S., "Jewish Ultra-Nationalism in Israel: Converging Strands," *Survey of Jewish Affairs 1985*, (Rutherford: Fairleigh Dickenson Press, 1985).

Liebman, Charles, and Don-Yehiya, Eliezer, *Civil Religion in Israel*, (Berkeley: University of California Press, 1983).

Lodge, David, *Changing Places*, (London: Martin Secker and Warburg, 1975).

Lofland, John, *Doomsday Cult*, (New York: Halstead Press, 1977).

Luckman, Thomas, *The Invisible Religion*, (New York: Macmillan, 1967).

Marcus, Ivan, *Piety and Society*, (Lieden: E.J. Brill, 1980).

Marsden, George M., *Fundamentalism and American Culture*, (New York: Oxford University Press, 1980).

Martin, David, *A General Theory of Secularization*, (Oxford: Basil Blackwell, 1978).

Martin, David, *The Religious and the Secular*, (New York: Schocken Books, 1969).

Marty, Martin, Review of *The Sacred in a Secular Age*, Robert Wuthnow, ed., *Journal for the Scientific Study of Religion*, 25 (September 1986) p. 376.

Massarik, Fred, "Affiliation and Non-Affiliation in the United States Jewish Community: A Reconceptualization," *American Jewish Year Book 1978*, (Philadelphia: Jewish Publication Society, 1978).

Mayer, Egon, *From Suburb to Shtetl: The Jews of Boro Park*, (Philadelphia: Temple University Press, 1979).

McCready, William C. with Greeley, Andrew M., *The Ultimate Values of the American Population*, (Beverly Hills: Sage, 1976).

Moore, Sally Falk, and Myerhoff, Barbara G., eds., *Secular Ritual*, (Assen/Amsterdam: Van Gorcum, 1977).

Neuhaus, John, ed., *Unsecular America*, (Grand Rapids, Michigan: William Eerdmans Publishing Co., 1986).

O'Dea, Thomas, "Five Dilemmas in the Institutionalization of Religion," *Journal for the Scientific Study of Religion*, 1 (Fall 1961), 30–39.

Oren, Dan, *Joining the Club: A History of Jews and Yale*, (New Haven: Yale University Press, 1985).

Phillips, Bruce, *Border Cities: Three Jewish Communities in the American West*, Forthcoming.

Rothschild, Joseph, *Ethnopolitics: A Conceptual Framework*, (New York: Columbia University Press, 1981).

Salmon, Yosef, "The Response of the Jewish Public to the Society for the Settlement of Eretz Israel," *Sefer Shraga*, Mordecai Eliav, and Yitzhak Rafael, eds., (Jerusalem: Mossad Harav Kook, in Hebrew, 1981).

Scherman, Rabbi Nosson, *The Family Zemiros*, (New York: Artscroll Mesorah Publications, 1981).

Schmeltz, Uziel, and DellaPergola, Sergio, "Some Basic Trends in the Demography of US Jews: a Reexamination," Paper prepared for a Conference on New Perspectives in American Jewish Sociology, American Jewish Committee, New York, 1986.

See, Katherine O'Sullivan, *First World Nationalisms*, (Chicago: University of Chicago Press, 1986).

Shaffir, William, "Witnessing as Identity Consolidation: The Case of the Lubavitcher Chassidim," *Identity and Religion*, Hans Mol, ed., (Beverly Hills, California: Sage, 1978).

Singer, David, "Living with Intermarriage," *Commentary*, 68 (July 1979), 52–4.

Sklare, Marshall, "The Jew in American Sociological Thought," *Ethnicity*, 1 (1974), 151–73.

Sklare, Marshall, "Jewish Acculturation and American Jewish Identity," *Jewish Life in America: Historical Perspectives*, Gladys Rosen, ed., (New York: Institute of Human Relations Press and Ktav, 1979).

Sklare, Marshall, and Greenblum, Joseph, *Jewish Identity on the Suburban Frontier*, (New York: Basic Books, 1967).

Smith, Anthony, *The Ethnic Revival*, (Cambridge: Cambridge University Press, 1981).

Smith, Donald, *Religion and Political Development*, (Boston: Little, Brown, 1970).

Trends, 11 (Spring 1986). Publication of the Jewish Education Service of North America.

Troeltsch, Ernst, *Social Teachings of the Christian Churches*, Two vols., (Chicago: University of Chicago Press, 1931).

Turner, Victor, *The Ritual Process*, (Chicago: Aldine, 1969).

Von der Mehden, Fred R., *Religion and Modernization in Southeast Asia*, (Syracuse: Syracuse University Press, 1986).

Waxman, Chaim, "The Limits of Futurology: Conflicting Perspectives on the American Jewish Community," *Survey of Jewish Affairs, 1986*, (Rutherford, N.J.: Fairleigh Dickenson Press, 1987).

Will There be One Jewish People by the Year 2000?, New York: The National Jewish Center for Learning and Leadership, "Critical Issues Conference," March 16–17 1986.

Williams, John, "Veiling in Egypt as a Political and Social Phenomenon," *Islam and Development*, John Esposito, ed., (Syracuse: Syracuse University Press, 1980).

Wilson, Bryan, *Contemporary Transformations of Religion*, (London: Oxford University Press, 1976)2.

Wilson, Bryan, *Magic and the Millenium*, (New York: Harper and Row,1973).

Wimberley, Ronald, C., "Dimensions of Commitment: Generalizing from Religion to Politics," *Journal for the Scientific Study of Religion*, 17 (September 1978), 225–40.

Woocher, Jonathan, *Sacred Survival: The Civil Religion of American Jews*, (Bloomington: Indiana University Press, 1986).

Wuthnow, Robert, ed., *The Sacred in a Secular Age*, (Berkeley: University of California Press, 1985).

York, Alan and Lazerwitz, Bernard, "Religious Involvement as the Main Gateway to Voluntary Association Activity," *Contemporary Jewry*, 8, (New Brunswick, N.J.: Transaction Books, 1987).

Index